Building Bridges of
Communication through
Point of Use Leadership

Building Bridges of Communication through Point of Use Leadership

Michael B Rall
J.C. Bridge Builders

ISBN: 0692427821
ISBN 13: 9780692427828
Library of Congress Control Number: 2015906647
J.C. Bridge Builders, Findlay, OH

In honor of the One who provides the way...

Jeremiah 29:11
"For I know the plans I have for you," declares the LORD, "plans to prosper you and not to harm you, plans to give you hope and a future".

Mark 10:43
"But among you it will be different. Whoever wants to be a leader among you must be your servant".

I want to thank my beautiful wife Carol, my two children Joshua and Ambelina, and my two great friends Frank and Will. They have been helping me with Building Bridges of Communication through Point of Use Leadership from concept to writing and publishing. Carol you have been unbelievably patient and supportive. I am grateful for every carpet picnic you ever had and every late night and early morning encouragement session. Joshua your willingness to intercede and fight for what was right, has meant the world to me. I truly enjoyed competing with you to see who would finish their book first almost as much as I enjoyed the scars and healings I received from your deeply needed editing! Ambelina, the combination of you caring heart and thoughtful approach towards your Dad and others has created some of the most helpful insights I have ever encountered. You are truly the most amazing Shelly I will ever meet! Frank, where would I be without your friendship and deep counsel? I shudder to think about it except maybe with your plans for Kate! Will, you are one of the most blessed men I have ever met. I am grateful for your humor, the boat, and for being included in your circle of friendship. There are many more friends, family, and colleagues that have helped me on this journey including Ha who pushed me to write this book. Your help and support have been invaluable. I am grateful.

Additional information or questions about Building Bridges of Communication through Point of Use Leadership can be found on our website at jcbridgebuilders.com or directed to jcbridgebuilders@gmail.com

Contents

Prologue

KATE BURSTS INTO Frank's office, making Frank jump at the sudden noise. "You know, Frank, I have had just about enough," she states with enough energy that Frank sits back in his chair, knowing this is one of those times that he needs to just listen. "I've tried everything I know to do, and it just isn't working." Kate begins pacing the room. Frank opens his mouth to ask a question, but Kate continues. "My people think I'm nuts," she says, throwing her arms up into the air in frustration, "and to be honest with you, I'm not sure they aren't right. One minute I think I have it figured out, and the next minute my whole world explodes!"

"Whoa, wait a minute, Kate. You may be a little nutty now and then, but you sound like you're going for the front of the class today. What's going on? What's got you so wound up?" Frank asks of his friend.

Kate slams down into one of the seats in front of Frank's desk. "It's this *empowerment* or *employee-engagement* thing—call it what you want—that we keep trying to implement. I've tried everything I know to help make it work, and every day it seems that I make it worse. And, you know, it isn't for lack of effort on my part or the people I work with. But it just seems that we have it wrong. In fact, most of the time, I just seem to make the people I work with angry—or, worse yet, they treat me like I'm trying to take advantage of them." She slumps back into the seat with a huff, putting her hand to her head. "I'd quit trying, but my gut tells me that it's the right idea, and I really *do* want it to work. I just don't know how."

Frank frowns and then nods in agreement. "I feel the same way," he admits. "I've just gotten to the point that I just keep going and pretend that we're happy and that we are all empowered employees. But in reality, I haven't been able to make heads or tails of it, myself. I know everyone says that we have to change the way we work together because business has changed and that we have to perform better and all that, but I don't see how it's all supposed to work together. Frankly I don't think I've ever seen it work."

Kate thinks for a moment. "Yeah, neither have I."

"I've heard the good stories," Frank continues.

"Me too," Kate says as she leans back in her chair for a moment, deep in thought.

"Every time I look for answers, all I get is mumbo jumbo on how it supposed to work," Frank says, breaking the silence and startling Kate slightly. "It's gotten to the point that every time I talk about it to my group, they just roll their eyes as if to say, 'Here it comes again.'" He leans back into his chair. "To be honest, I'm ready to go back to the other way and just tell everyone what to do and how to do it. At least then I'd know what to expect. And the older guys seem to be more comfortable that way too. They haven't liked me much since I became a supervisor, but they say at least before this empowerment thing I was a *consistent* pain in the neck...or somewhere lower."

Kate grins. "Now that I think about it, you *were* consistent."

Frank shoots her a look. "Thanks."

Kate nods. "Mm-hmm." She sighs, and both sit quietly again for a few moments. "But really, I have to figure this out before I lose my mind, along with my interest. If we don't figure it out soon, our operations manager is going to try to blame me and anyone else who has even looked at trying to make this work for all the performance issues he has in his work areas. He's been looking for a reason to get rid of our employee-empowerment effort for quite a while. And some of the time, he acts like we're out to get him personally."

Frank scoffs. "You noticed it too?"

"I think I almost understand why he feels that way," Kate says, "but I don't want to give up. Almost everyone agrees that empowerment, or at least the concept of it, is the right thing to do, but trying to do it is just about killing it."

"Well, what can we do?" Frank asks. "We've done just about all we can think of, right?"

Kate nods in agreement, and the two are quiet again. Kate stares out the window at the lawn just outside Frank's office window. *Honestly,* Kate thinks to herself, *all I want is for the weekend to get here faster so I can be at...*her eyes widen as a realization dawns on her. She sits up. "You know, Frank, tomorrow afternoon I'm leaving to see Joshua."

Frank looks at her and frowns in confusion. "Your good friend from college that you worked with years ago?"

Kate nods. "Yeah."

"I didn't know that you two were still connected. I haven't heard you talk about him for a while," he says.

"No, but we've been keeping in touch, just maybe not as much lately. We were getting together at least once a year and talking more than that, but lately, with family and work, we've found it a little more difficult to find time," Kate tells Frank. "But that's not the point. The point is, we are getting together to talk, and maybe he'll let me bend his ear a little about this empowerment thing. He used to be one of those hard-charging command-and-control kind of guys, but then he got all wrapped up in the people side of the business. He's been working through his own company helping businesses and community organizations ever since."

"What's he doing with community organizations, taking the easy way out?" Frank jokes.

Kate grimaces. "You and I both know that leading in a volunteer or non-profit organization is sometimes a heck of a lot harder than leading in a traditional for-profit company," she retorts. "No, he isn't taking the easy way out. He's still driven to help people succeed, and he's been helping all kinds of organizations improve their performance and success."

"Sounds like the help we could use," Frank says. "Did he say what changed?"

"I never really listened. He said he has a different perspective now and that he approaches things much differently than we did in the old days. I looked up a couple of interviews once that reporters did with some of the people he's helped, and they say they love him like he's family, as well as loving their newfound success. He's been trying to tell me about the changes he's gone through for a couple of years now, but I just keep putting him off."

"You mean we could have had answers before now?" Frank half teases.

"Huh," Kate says, looking thoughtful. "Yeah, right. I guess it's time we talked about it."

Frank waits to see if Kate will elaborate, but she continues to stare off, lost in thought. An argument breaks out on the floor, and both Kate and Frank look to see Tom and Mara and a few others gathered around one of the machines. Kate and Frank can hear a little of the conversation—enough to know that they're arguing about a process that isn't working well. Frank sighs and gets up to go out to help. He stops at the door. "Well, you go talk to him and see if he has any answers, and I'll see if I can keep the fires under control while you're gone. Sound like a deal?"

Kate smiles sympathetically at Frank. "Sounds good to me."

CHAPTER 1

Overview

IN CHAPTER 1, Kate goes to see her friend Joshua and discusses with him her struggles with implementing empowerment and creating employee engagement. Joshua asks Kate several questions that lead her to a deeper understanding of how the impacts of the current business environment are creating a shift in focus from management to leadership.

CHAPTER 1

Transitions from Management to Leadership
Livin' Large in Dilbertville
Realizing the Drivers of Change

As KATE DRAWS closer to Joshua's home, she tries to focus her thoughts on how much she is looking forward to catching up with her longtime friend, but she just can't quite stifle the hope that maybe she can get some solutions to her struggles at work. She sighs as she pulls into Joshua's driveway, puts her car in park, and shuts it off. She thinks about their friendship for a moment. She and Joshua had become great friends in college. They had helped each other get through the first tough years of entering the workforce, they were there for each other when they met their future spouses, and they even attended each other's weddings. They had always had a great time talking about business and life, and their shared sense of humor had always given them an advantage in working through challenging times and developing creative solutions.

She takes a deep breath. *I'll work at getting to the problems,* she tells herself, *but first, this is about seeing a friend.* She gets out of the car and walks up the front-porch steps. She knocks on the door, and her mind takes off again at a million miles an hour with the questions she wants to ask about the business. She looks around at the scenery, trying to soak up the peace that seems to surround Joshua's house: the glow of the lawn in the light of early dusk, and the gentle light glowing from the front window.

Joshua opens the door, making Kate jump. She is surprised to see that he seems to look younger than the last time they had seen each other. He is relaxed and smiles at her reaction. He extends a warm handshake to her and then hugs her. As he steps back to invite her in, he looks into her eyes with the same penetrating gaze she remembers from their first meeting. Over the years, the focused way that Joshua always had of looking into someone's eyes had made Kate and others a little uncomfortable at times, but this time Kate just smiles back and asks, "Well, partner, do you see anything new?"

"Well, you look a little tense around the gills," he tells her, laughing a little.

Kate smiles sheepishly. "Is it that noticeable?" She walks in, and Joshua closes the door behind them. Kate begins to take off her coat. "I do feel that if I was any more wired, I'd be able to light up half the town on Christmas Eve, but I was hoping it showed a little less."

"Well, why don't you sit down, relax, and make yourself at home? I'll get us something to drink and a little something to eat while we talk." Kate nods and heads over to one of the empty chairs in the living room while Joshua goes into the kitchen.

She drapes her coat over the back of her chair and then sits down. She tries to calm down again by looking around but struggles to maintain any kind of focus. Fortunately, Joshua comes out a just a few seconds later with a tray that has a couple glasses of iced tea, some chips and dip in containers, and a couple of small plates. "Well, my old friend, what's got you so wired?" he asks as he sets the tray down on the coffee table.

"You mean you just want to jump right in?" Kate asks as Joshua sits down. "You sure you don't want to talk about the good stuff first, like how the kids are doing, the wife, the dog, the car?"

Joshua smiles, trying to suppress a laugh. "I'm afraid that if we don't talk about it now, we won't make it through the good stuff."

Kate smiles sheepishly again. "OK, fine. You got me. But let's make sure we leave time to talk about the rest later, OK? I don't want this to be all business. I'm crazy enough thinking about it all the time as it is."

Joshua takes a drink of his iced tea and nods. "So why don't you start at the beginning and fill me in."

Joshua settles back into the couch as Kate begins to explain about the challenges at work and about her conversation with Frank the day before. When she's done, she asks, "So what do you think?"

"Well, I think you and Frank have a really good start on solving your problems and making good decisions," he answers.

"We do? How?"

"You're asking a lot of good questions."

"You really think the questions are helping? I thought all those questions were causing half the problems," she says.

Joshua nods in understanding. "In a management culture, or a place where the focus is on maintaining the status quo, questions can be a little frustrating. But, not to give you a big head, asking questions is what good leaders do," he tells her.

"And so by asking questions that means I'm a leader? I mean, I have a million of them, so I must be on my way to becoming a great leader, right?" Kate asks, smiling a little but unsure of where the conversation is going.

"I'm sure you'll be a great leader someday," Joshua says reassuringly, "but let's start things out a little more slowly."

Kate takes a sip of her iced tea, puts some chips and dip on one of the small plates, and sits back. "OK, so I'll start out easy on myself. What do you mean when you say there's a change from management to leadership? I've heard it, like everyone else, but I can't see the difference."

"That's part of the struggle, Kate. Most people, and their organizations, can't tell the difference either. We know management really well, and we can agree on the definition of management for the most part and how we expect people to manage. But people are really having a hard coming up with a common definition for *leadership*, which is what makes it difficult to help others understand what you want or expect from them."

"You make it sound like you can see the difference, though," Kate points out, a hopeful tone in her voice. "And are you willing to share with the class?"

He sets down his tea and sits up. "I see what I believe are the differences, Kate. I think an easy way to explain the differences would be for me to share a perspective on how I feel management got started, why I think we are moving into an era of leadership today, and what leadership is."

Kate rolls her eyes. "Oh, great…a story. And here I thought I was just going to get the bullet points," she says jokingly.

Joshua smiles at the business joke and starts explaining. "The concept for starting up a business has always been pretty much the same," he begins. "Someone would come up with a product or a service that people wanted or needed and were willing to pay for. When they figured out how they wanted to make the product or provide the service, they would set up their business. As the business grew, they would hire people to make sure they made as many products, or provided as many people with the service, as possible. Once the owner came up with the best process for making and selling as many of the widgets or services as possible, the last thing he or she wanted people to do was to change that successful process. So owners hired managers to make sure that the process didn't change and the business ran the same way every day. That way, no one would mess up their cash cow

"If they were lucky or had good business insight and ability, the demand for the widget or service would increase, and they would often create another business at a different location, just like the first one. And then they would hire more managers to make sure the new business was run the same way."

"Sounds like success to me," Kate says. "So when did the headaches start?"

"Oh, they showed up soon enough," Joshua says. "When they were looking for a new manager or supervisor, they either hired from the outside or they promoted people from within. In either case, they were looking for people who knew how to make sure that the processes were set up and that they ran the same way every day. Frequently, the people they promoted from inside the business were the best at running the machines or services themselves. The thought was, who would be better to help the people run the processes the right way every day than someone who was already the best at running them? Most of the job was to make sure that everyone ran the processes the way they were originally set up to run. If they weren't running the machine or service that way, then the supervisor or manager was expected to show them or tell them how to do the job the right way."

"So the idea was that they were experts," Kate summarizes, "and that they would be good at showing people how to run the job the best way, right?" She grabs some more chips and dip and puts them on her plate as she sits back and waits for Joshua's answer.

"You're right, Kate, but the problem was that most of the conversations that managers and supervisors had with the process owners occurred only when something had gone wrong with the process. The goal was to take it back to the way it was supposed to be running. So the supervisor or manager would explain what was wrong to the process owners and then show them how to do it correctly.

Kate reflects for a moment on her own experiences at work. "They must not have had a lot of friends."

"What makes you say that?" Joshua asks.

"You can't tell your friends—or even strangers—that they're wrong all the time and expect them to want to work with you, let alone talk to you," Kate says. She squirms uneasily in her chair, thinking about some of the conversations she's had at work recently.

"That's a good observation Kate. It does take a toll on relationships when the majority of conversations that you have with someone are about what you haven't done correctly."

But she feels as if something else isn't being addressed and is having a hard time putting it into words. Finally, she says, "But it's not as if us managers and supervisors have had it any easier."

"That's true," Joshua agrees. "The management model caused a lot of problems on the supervisor and manager side as well. They were hired or promoted with the expectation that they knew everything about the jobs or processes in those areas, and what they did not know they would quickly learn. Along with that, they were held accountable for knowing what was going on all the time in their departments, with the expectation that everything could and would be fixed right away."

"And usually before anyone had a chance to see what had happened or ask any questions," Kate says with a frustrated look on her face.

"Over time, the management approach led to several problems."

Kate scoffs. "Just a few," she says as stares into her glass of iced tea.

Joshua smiles with sympathy at his friend, remembering all the problems he had before things changed for him. "Since they were expected to know all of the answers and were giving most of the answers all day long to the process owners, after a while many managers began to believe and behave as if they *were* the only ones who had the right answers. This led to managers and supervisors not trusting or valuing the input of those who worked for them. After a while, because the majority of the conversations with employees were about how to do the job right and frequently showing them how to do the job, most businesses and organizations came to the conclusion that they just couldn't find good employees anymore."

"Makes sense that conflict management is always at the top of the list for training," Kate says. "First they tell the people who work for them, whether they're old friends or complete strangers, that they don't know what they're doing, and then they ignore their ideas for doing things better."

"The hard part was that they really thought they were doing the right thing and couldn't understand why everyone was so angry. So they just toughened themselves up, believing that this was the way it had to be for them to be able to help the company, and the people who worked for them, to be successful." Joshua pauses for a moment and then continues. "I've seen a lot of my good friends take on a management role, only to become frustrated as their friendships broke down with those they used to work with and now were managing."

"So why didn't they go to college and learn something better?" Kate asks, trying to change the direction of the conversation so that she can quit thinking about how she has been managing. "Things have changed so much."

"Well, that's another part of the problem," Joshua explains. "After years of seeing many businesses become successful with a management approach, most universities, including almost all of the best, started management programs based on what they had observed and believed would work best. These observations were made at what were considered the best companies, which were the ones that had prospered in stable market economies. The universities and colleges taught the management way until it was considered the only way. Because management became the accepted way of running organizations, it got into our community organizations and schools as well."

Kate frowns. "What do you mean?"

"Because many successful businesspeople were respected in the community for organizing companies and making them run, they were given positions of influence or authority in schools, churches, and community organizations. Naturally they used the management techniques they had learned at work with the intent of helping. And as this influence grew, it even became a way of parenting as well."

Kate shifts uncomfortably in her chair again and looks at the floor. "So pretty soon everyone is focusing on what people are doing wrong? Even at home?" She begins to feel frustrated as her mind drifts to interactions she has seen in community organizations and school-improvement efforts and, even more saddening, interactions she's had with her daughter at home.

"Not everyone all the time, Kate," Joshua quickly encourages. Kate looks up and smiles at the gesture. "But enough that it became a way of life or a culture of management, as we've called it, in many areas."

"So when did somebody notice that we needed to change?" Kate asks.

"For the most part, it wasn't until many companies and their people had experienced a shift from working in stable, long-term markets to ones that were that were global, short term, and ever changing that the management culture was challenged."

"What do you mean stable and ever-changing markets? And what happened to make the change?"

"In general, what happened was that the governments of many countries decided that the best way to help maintain steady economies and governments was to have free trade between countries. Staying away from whether or not we agree with the approach and whether or not it is working, the effect was that many competitors for products and services started to show up from all over the world. The first impact was that it drove a need in many companies to very quickly change and improve so that they could stay in business."

"Ah, that one I have experienced." Kate nods with understanding.

"A second impact was that, most often, when businesses only had to compete within their home country or even just a region of a country, there weren't too many changes to deal with. It only required decisions every now and then, which most often only came from the highest levels. But when competition started coming from multiple directions almost all the time, it required changes in every part of the business, also almost all the time, to be able to compete.

"While the demand of competition used to be slow and affected only a small group of people, now it affected every level of the business: from individual process owners running machines to the supervisors and managers providing services to executive administrative assistants providing data to executives. Everyone had to consider how his or her processes were contributing positively to the current needs of both the customers and the company.

Everyone was being pushed to figure out how to get from a state that wasn't working as efficiently or as effectively as needed to a state that would."

"On the surface, that doesn't sound so bad," Kate says. "Competition causes the need for us to improve at every level and drives everyone to come up with a plan to go forward and do better, right?"

"By itself, change is challenging enough, but a major problem was that everyone had become so used to only a few people making decisions in the management culture for so long that very few people were ready to provide the leadership that was needed to go forward successfully."

"Yeah, but I thought that we eventually learned that we needed leadership. It's all over the papers and magazines," Kate says, holding up one of the magazines on Joshua's coffee table. "And not just for businesses. It's needed in community organizations, schools, government—you name it. Amber's been to more than a few seminars at her school about leadership."

"You're right. We did learn. When we began to encounter change frequently and began to notice the strain, we knew that we needed leadership, but we couldn't figure out why things weren't working when we tried to do it."

"Is it because everybody's still focusing on management?" Kate asks. "Because that's what it seems like to me."

"That's a significant part of the problem, yes," Joshua answers. "But just as challenging was the fact that no one was able to clearly explain what leadership was or what the process of leadership was. Up to this point, a manager's job had been to maintain the status quo by stating the facts as they knew them and bring things back to the original baseline."

"Now executives were suddenly asking their people to go forward. But in order to do that—in order to be able to make good decisions on how to go forward to a better future state—you need to have good information, not only about where you are now but also about where you need to be and the steps you need to take to get there."

Kate leans back in her chair, frowning thoughtfully. "Don't managers and supervisors already know all that?"

"Most are trained and skilled at knowing how to get *back* to where they were, not at figuring out how to help themselves or others go forward," Joshua tells her. "That requires a different set of ideas and information and requires a different process."

"Are we talking about leadership?"

"We are, Kate. Let me show you a couple of visuals about leadership." He places them on the coffee table. "The first visual shows that leadership requires that we shift from making statements about where we are, or where we were, to asking the right questions about where we need to be and how we can get there. When we need to change," Joshua continues, "or to transition from a current state to a better future state, need to ask the right questions in the right sequence. This makes it possible for us to gather the best information possible, within the time and resource constraints that we have, to make the best decisions possible."

Stable Market Economy	Changing Market Economy
Traditional Organization	Operational Excellence Organization

Lead

Plan, Organize, and Control

Management

Implement: Workforce

Workforce Leadership:

Plan, Lead, Organize, and Control

Webster's definitions:

Management: The act of controlling...

Leadership: To go with or ahead to show the way...

Stating Facts about the Past

Asking Questions for the Future

JC Bridge Builders © 2013

"Aha!" Kate states excitedly. "I knew I was on the right track by asking so many questions." Joshua smiles questioningly at his friend, and she rolls her eyes. "OK, maybe I wasn't so sure, but…," she pauses, thinking back to her recent experiences, "I believe at least I was headed in the right direction by trying to help my group to go forward to something better."

"And you're right, Kate," Joshua affirms. "Leadership, or the goal of leadership shown in this second visual, demonstrates that in its simplest form, leadership is helping yourself, or someone else, transition from an unwanted or unneeded current state to a better future state."

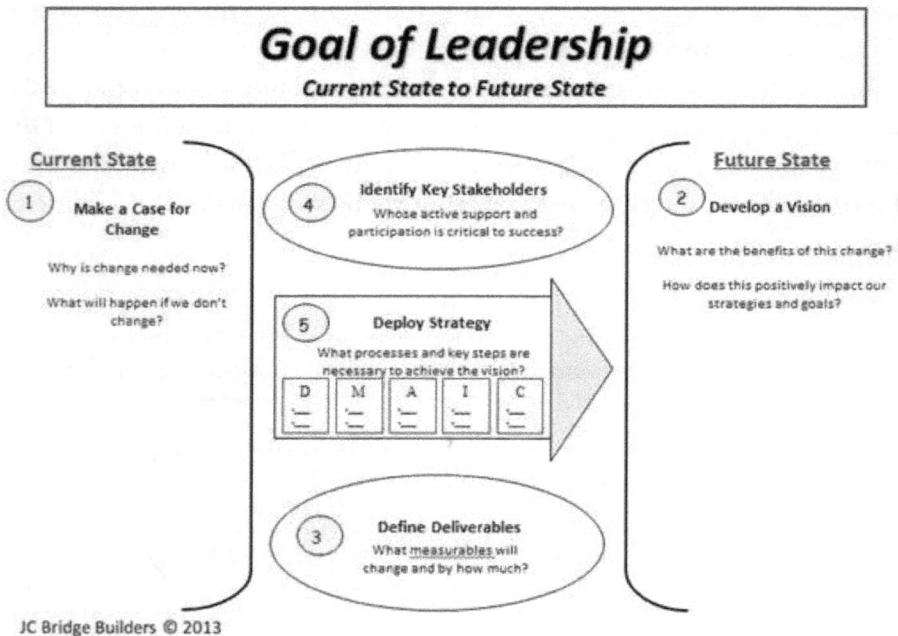

Goal of Leadership
Current State to Future State

Current State

1 Make a Case for Change

Why is change needed now?

What will happen if we don't change?

4 **Identify Key Stakeholders** Whose active support and participation is critical to success?

5 **Deploy Strategy** What processes and key steps are necessary to achieve the vision?

D	M	A	I	C

3 **Define Deliverables** What measurables will change and by how much?

Future State

2 Develop a Vision

What are the benefits of this change?

How does this positively impact our strategies and goals?

JC Bridge Builders © 2013

"Well, when you put it that way," Kate says, again thinking of what she's been doing with her group at work, "it makes sense that my first instinct in trying to help my group go forward was to start asking questions. But honestly, so far I feel like I've been asking mostly random questions." She looks up at Joshua hopefully. "You said that we needed to ask the right questions in the right sequence to provide leadership. Can we talk about those questions today?"

Joshua smiles gently. "We could, but remember when you said you wanted to leave time to talk about the good stuff?"

"You bet," Kate says, turning to look at the clock hanging on the living room wall. "Wow," she comments, seeing the time, "it's later than I thought."

"I think we discussed a lot of concepts and ideas today, Kate, and if you want, we can get together again sometime soon and talk some more."

She sighs. "OK, fine. But one last work question. What does any of this management-to-leadership stuff have to do with empowerment and employee engagement? Isn't that where we started?"

"You are right, that is where we started, but how about we save that one for next time too," Joshua offers, "because that may require a lengthy conversation as well."

"Aw, come on," she teases. "Pretty please?"

Joshua grins and continues forward. "How soon do you want to meet?"

"I'm pretty sure I'll have some free time next weekend, if that will work for your schedule, but I'll have to check first and let you know for sure."

"Sounds good to me," Joshua says. "Meanwhile, I would like you to think about what we discussed. You know how important I feel it is to internalize a concept by comparing it to your own experiences."

"Yeah, yeah, I remember." Kate says, rolling her eyes as she remembers the debates and discussions they had over the differences between what they had learned in college and what they had seen and experienced when translating and applying those ideas in the workplace. Joshua had always compared the difference to memorizing and stating facts versus doing word problems or answering essay questions, the latter of which Kate had despised.

"And don't just compare them to your experiences at work, but at home and in your community also," Joshua adds.

She puts her hands together in mock prayer and bows, "Yes, Master Joshua."

"Very good, my young pupil. You will learn quickly," Joshua teases back. "Now tell me the good stuff, grasshopper. How has life been in your personal path?"

Chapter 1 Work

Monday morning, Kate makes her way toward Frank's office to see if her friend is in, eager to share her discussion with Joshua. What she wants to know is if what she heard resonates with Frank's experiences as much as it does with hers.

As Kate comes up to the doorway to Frank's office, she sees a frustrated Frank talking to one of his employees, Julie. "Look, it's important for you to behave like a leader if you want to move up the ladder," he is explaining to her.

Julie puts her hand on her hips. "And how's that?" she asks tartly. "How does a leader behave, Frank, and what exactly is a leader supposed to be doing?"

Frank fumbles for an answer, clearly unable to explain it himself. Finally he tells her, "I don't know how to describe it, but I'll know it when I see it."

Julie scoffs and rolls her eyes. "Well, when you get smart enough to tell me what it is you want me to do, I'll do it." She turns to leave the office, "If that's what you really want, that is." She walks briskly out of Frank's office, and Kate moves to get out of her way.

Frank throws himself back into his chair and groans.

"Well," Kate says as she walks up to Frank's desk. "That could've gone better."

Frank sighs. "Yeah, no kidding." He sits up and looks at Kate. "It might actually be funny if I was the only one in the dark here. Except I get the same kind of answer from everyone else I talk to, including Molly in our human resources group."

Kate frowns and sits down across from Frank. "What do you mean?"

"In my succession-planning reviews, she is always telling me that I'm managing well and that I'll make a great leader someday," Frank tells her. "She says nothing ever gets too out of control in the areas I'm responsible for and that they can depend on me to keep things the way they should be. But when I ask about what is expected of me as a leader, she starts shifting around like I'm asking her to walk on a bed of hot coals."

Kate smiles. "And you would know how someone should act when walking across hot coals?"

"Funny, Kate," he shoots back. "Anyway, most of the time, the way people explain it, it seems like being a leader is the same as being a manager, but she says it's different. She usually says something about exhibiting leadership attributes or something like that, but when I ask her just to tell me what a leader does, that's usually about the time the conversation ends." Frank puts his head in his hands and begins pulling at his hair. "At this rate, I'll probably never know what leadership really is or what I'm supposed to be doing to become a good leader."

Kate grins. Frank looks up at her and frowns. "What are you smiling about? That's not helpful, Kate."

"Tell you what, Frank," Kate says, "how about I treat you to a double shot of espresso right after work. We can stop for a few minutes, and I can share with you what Joshua and I talked about over the weekend."

Frank smiles. "I could definitely use something after what I've been through this morning. And if that look in your eye is anything to go on, I feel like I just might want to hear this."

Kate nods in agreement. "I think what he said could really give you some ideas for helping Julie get the promotion that you want her to have."

"More importantly, will it keep her from verbally abusing me?" Frank asks.

"Oh, I don't know about that, Frank. We pay her a lot to keep you on the ropes. It wouldn't be fair to take away her second income," she says innocently.

"Oh great," Frank laments. "How much? Can I give a counteroffer?"

"It's more than you can afford, mi amigo," Kate says with a deadpan expression. "And believe me—we would outbid you anyway. The entertainment factor is worth it to us."

"Us? Who's 'us'?"

Kate gets up and heads toward the door. "See you at the coffeehouse, Frank."

Later as Kate and Frank are sitting at the local café, Kate tells Frank what Joshua shared with her about the differences between management and leadership.

As Kate raises her cup to take a drink, she asks, "So what do you think?"

Frank thinks for a moment and then says, "Well, the good news is that at times I have been doing what a leader does, but the bad news is that now that I know what it is, I'm not sure I know how to do it very well. On top of that, I see that I spend most of my time managing Julie and the others by almost always asking them to put things back the way they were instead of letting her and the groups go forward. The worst part for me is that what has been aggravating me the most is all the questions Julie was asking. Most of the time I thought she was just wasting time."

Kate nods. "I understand, Believe me. I've been having a lot of the same type of thoughts."

Frank pauses for a moment and then gets an impish grin on his face. "Would you like to hear the really good stuff, though? I saved it for last."

"That smile usually means trouble for me, Frank," Kate says. She grabs her cup for another drink. "But for the sake of curiosity, what's the really good stuff?"

"I thought you'd never ask." He sets his cup down excitedly. "The really good news is that now that I know the difference between management and leadership and have done some leadership, I can finally tell my new boss," he pauses, indicating Kate, "that I'm ready for a promotion."

Kate almost spits out her coffee and begins coughing. "Wait a minute, Frank," she says, waving him off to let him know she is going to be OK. Kate coughs a couple of times and smiles gamely as she tries to regain control. Finally she calms down and tries again. "Hold your horses there, cowboy. We may know what a leader is now, and we've done a little work with the concept, but maybe we should look around first and try to understand it and get a little more practice being leaders before one of us asks to be the next CEO."

"Aw, you're no fun, Kate," Frank says jokingly. "Well, maybe. But I'm not sure near-death experiences are supposed to be fun."

Kate sighs and smiles. "I'm OK, Frank, but how about if you were to talk with Julie and see what she thinks of all this?"

Frank frowns at the idea of having another conversation so soon with Julie.

"She has a pretty good head on her shoulders," Kate continues, "and I would be interested to know what she thinks, especially with her position in the company."

"I know you're right, Kate," he admits, "and I promise to talk to her. But still, I hear there might be a big promotion coming, and I want to get my hat in the ring."

"Great, Frank, you're making me nervous," Kate says. "How about talking with Julie first and then stopping by tomorrow afternoon to let me know how it went."

"You're such a killjoy, Kate. Don't you want me to wear a new hat?" Frank asks as he pretends to try on a new hat.

"Sure I do," Kate tells him, "I just want to make sure it's going to fit first. It's important, you know."

Frank rolls his eyes, smiling.

"One other small detail, though. Once you've explained to Julie what leadership is, how would you explain to her how it works? Let alone explaining all this to Molly in human resources."

Frank pauses. "Fine, if you're going to start asking logical questions…" Frank trails off and then smiles. "OK, you're a good friend, Kate, so maybe not this week, but definitely after I get done talking to Julie I should go see her."

"That's enough, Frank!" Kate says, smiling. She turns to the waitress and signals for the check.

Two days later, Julie listens as Frank explains to her what Kate told him in the café. Kate sits nearby, waiting. A smile breaks out on Julie's face. "You know, Frank, all those things we say about you aren't true. But I'm not giving any of the money back, because Kate says I can't or else." She winks at Kate.

Kate smiles, realizing that Julie must've heard her in the hall.

"Wait, what things?" Frank asks, looking alarmed.

"In any case," Julie continues, ignoring Frank's question, "thanks for finally explaining about management and leadership. I think we can use what you're saying to help on that old job in the corner, as it needs to go from its current malfunctioning state to a much better performing future state. Though I don't think it will take very much of an investment to make it a lot better," she adds.

"How do you know that?" Frank asks, confused and a little surprised that Julie knows what to do.

"You know all those questions I've been asking? A few of them were aimed at understanding how the operators did their jobs and the same with the maintenance group, but most of them were focused on the process itself. I got the lowdown on what it would take to get this thing running again."

"Really?" Frank's eyes widen in amazement.

"You just have to know the right questions," she says teasingly.

"Great," he says. "Well, do you guys have a monopoly on the questions or how to know what questions to ask? Maybe you could share with your boss a little."

"Well, maybe for a price," she says looking up at the ceiling like she's thinking it over. "You know, it's all about the money." Kate and Julie laugh. When they calm down, Julie says, "In all seriousness, Frank, you know I would be happy to share what I know with you, but I don't have a set of questions or a process I follow or anything like that. I just ask what I think are the right questions at the right time."

Frank nods. "I hear you. But any insight you can offer would be better than where I am at the moment. How about I bring a couple of gold bars and maybe you can share a few pearls of wisdom with me? Does that sound like a deal?"

Julie again looks like she's thinking it over. "Well, I prefer burritos to gold bullion, especially during lunch. And I'm not sure gold is equal to pearls." She laughs and stands up. "But I will see you tomorrow, Frank, and we'll see what we can do. And thanks for calling me in."

"Thanks for not coming in loaded for bear," Frank offers up, relieved.

Julie laughs and heads out of Frank's office.

Kate shakes her head and smiles. "You know, this is some of the best news I've heard in a while. I'm not any surer than Julie is on how to approach leadership other than by just asking questions as I think of them, but it sounds like we're on the right track." She scoots her seat across from Frank. "You know, I can't wait to hear how Joshua ties this in with empowerment."

Frank nods absently. "I think that the questions feel right, too. And Julie looked like she'd been waiting for years to have this conversation." He looks up at Kate. "Wait, what do you mean Joshua is going to tie this in with empowerment? Can't we just solve one mystery at a time?"

Kate shrugs. "Well, I'm with you on that. But maybe that's what has been getting in the way." She stands up and stretches. "I'm heading up to Joshua's again this weekend. I'll run the questions and empowerment thing by him and talk to you about it on Monday. It's nice to finally have someone to bounce these ideas off, you know?"

"Oh, I see. Now I don't exist," Frank pouts. "Your old friend is the only one you can talk to, is he?"

Kate laughs. "Frank, that's not what I mean, and you know it. Though if there's something I can do to make you feel better about yourself, just let me know."

"Well, I prefer double espressos and doughnuts in the morning," Frank says, standing up and smiling. "I'm sure that should heal some of the wounds."

Kate rolls her eyes as the pair of them head out of his office.

Chapter 1 Home

When Kate gets home that evening, she heads toward the kitchen to begin making some dinner for herself. As she turns the corner, she sees her seventeen year old daughter, Amber, standing at the counter making a sandwich. Seeing Amber reminds her of an earlier conversation she had with her husband, David. She sighs. "You know, Amber, you sure put me in a tough spot the other day with your father," she says as she opens the pantry to see what's available. "In fact, you got to him so much that he finally cracked and said he wants you to be totally responsible for your own life."

Amber scoffs and rolls her eyes. "Oh yeah? What does that mean, more rules?" she asks as she turns to put the bread back in the cupboard.

Kate pauses for a moment and reflects on her conversation with Joshua and what she has seen during the past few days at work with Frank and Julie. *Well, it couldn't hurt to ask*, she thinks to herself. She turns to her daughter. "Hey, Amber," she calls.

Amber turns toward her. "Yeah?" she asks warily.

"You know, we've given you all the rules that you need to know about what actions you should and shouldn't take. And we have always let you know when you weren't meeting them and how to get back to choosing the right actions and doing them, right?"

Amber leans back against the counter and sighs. "More than you know, Mom," she says with a little bit of sarcasm.

Kate smiles sympathetically. "Fair enough. So let's talk about what I would like from you going forward."

"Oh, great. Like I thought—more rules," Amber grumbles.

"No sweetie, not rules. As I said, I think we have enough of those," she says encouragingly. "My hope is that we can start out with you telling me what you think you would like to be doing in the next three to five years."

"You gotta be kidding, Mom!" Amber almost cries out. "I don't have any plans yet for this weekend or know if I'm even going to have a weekend. How am I supposed to know what I'm going to be doing in the next three to five years? Is this some new torture method to test me and see if I can mess up my future too? You and Dad have demonstrated great control over my life and the great skill of knowing all my flaws."

Kate frowns, suddenly realizing the similarities between conversations at work and at home. "I'm sorry, Amber," she says finally. "That's honestly not what we were trying to do. And it's not what I'm trying to do now. I really just wanted to know what you wanted to do with your future and see if I might be able to help." She sits down at the kitchen table and sighs. "I think we may have managed way too long here too," she says to herself.

"What do you mean, 'managed'?" Amber asks. She makes her way over to her mom, seeing the hurt expression on Kate's face. "Hey," she says apologetically, "I'm sorry for losing it. I'm just kind of frustrated right now because I don't know what to do. It feels like everyone is asking me what I'm going to do with my life, and to be honest, even though I'm a senior in high school, I really haven't given it much thought. I've pretty much been told what to do since first grade, and now everyone wants me to turn on some magic switch and know how to plan out my future, like I've had practice at it or something. I mean, is there some secret society I don't know about where you get answers for that?"

Kate smiles and puts a reassuring hand on her daughter's. "No, sweetie. Not yet, anyway." Amber smiles in confusion at the "not yet" part of the statement. Kate continues, "But I think I might have a friend who can help."

"Who is that?"

"I'm not sure if you would remember him. We worked together when you were a lot younger. He used to visit all the time, but then he moved and…"

"You mean Joshua?" Amber asks. "Is that who you went to see this weekend?"

Kate blinks with some surprise. "I didn't think you would remember him."

"I liked him," Amber says. "He seemed a little rough at times when it came to talking about people and problems in the business, but you guys seemed to work it out. Plus, you always seemed to have a good time and you used to smile and laugh a lot more about business when you talked with him." Kate thinks about Amber's comments and wonders again why she put off talking to Joshua about business for so long.

"So—what—does he have the secret handshake or something that can help us out?" Amber asks, which brings Kate back from her thoughts.

"No, but he gave me some ideas about managing and leading," Kate tells her.

"Ah, so that's what your comment was about," Amber says. Kate nods. "What did you mean when you said that you've managed way too long here?"

Kate starts to explain, but Amber stops her. "Wait, this isn't going to take too long, is it? I mean, I do have friends coming over soon." She comments with hope in her voice while trying to make a point.

Kate laughs. "OK, I get the hint," she says. "The short version is that instead of teaching you how to ask the right questions so that you could learn how to be successful and overcome problems or make decisions on your own, your father and I have just been giving you rules and telling you how to follow them. And when you made mistakes, we told you what you had done wrong and how to do it right."

Amber nods thoughtfully. "Yeah, that's pretty much how I remember it too. Not that you guys aren't loving parents or anything."

Kate smiles. "Thanks, Amber."

"No problem," Amber teases.

"Anyway, it's just that we've spent a lot of years just focusing on what you were doing wrong and not helping you to get better or recognizing how much you already knew and had done successfully," Kate explains.

"We weren't trying to be mean or discouraging. We were honestly trying to help you be successful. But I'm not too happy at the moment with how we went about it. Your father says all the time that it isn't *what* you're saying—it's *how*." Kate grins with chagrin. "It's so frustrating when he's right."

"I feel your pain there, Mom." Amber chuckles. "But I promise not to tell." Kate laughs with Amber. "I'm not sure I get all of what you're saying, but I do have to come up with a plan for college soon, and I really could use some help. I have a ton of questions, and I don't even know where to start."

"I'll be glad to help," Kate says. "And I'm sorry."

Amber shrugs. "I know you love me, Mom. You and Dad have always been there for me, even when we didn't agree. Maybe we can talk again sometime? My Sunday afternoons aren't too crowded right now. If you would like, I can pencil you in."

Kate smiles. "Ha-ha. Thanks, sweetie. I would love that, actually. I'll have my people contact your people, and we'll work something out."

The doorbell rings, and Amber gets up from the table.

"Sounds good, Mom. I'll see you later," she says as she grabs her sandwich and heads out the door.

CHAPTER 2

Overview

IN CHAPTER 2, Joshua asks Kate why she is trying to create empowerment and what it is that she wants from her employees when she asks for empowerment.

Kate comes to the realization that what she really is asking for when she asks for empowerment is leadership.

CHAPTER 2

Leadership and Empowerment
*Who's on First? What's on Second?
If We Want Leadership, Why Are
We Asking for Empowerment?*

It is almost dark when Kate finally reaches Joshua's house, a few traffic jams slowing her progress along the way. The porch light greets her on her way up the driveway, and Kate feels a sense of relief, as well as anticipation, at finally making it to her friend's house. She is eager to pick up last week's conversation, especially after seeing how even a small application of what Joshua had to say could make such a difference.

Joshua waves from the garage and hangs a rake up on the wall. As Kate gets out of her car, Joshua closes the garage door and walks up to greet her. "Perfect timing," he says as they hug and begin walking toward the house. Joshua opens the door, and Kate is greeted by the smell of hot chocolate. As Kate looks towards the living room table she sees that Joshua had put out two mugs of hot chocolate and two plates, one with chocolates on it, and the other with different types of fruit.

Kate grins. "Well, although I was grateful for the chips and dip, this is a nice improvement! Has Lisa been involved?"

"Yes, I have been chastised by my wife about the proper treatment of guests at the house," Joshua tells her. "I was forced to put out good snacks as well as my favorites. Lisa told me that most people are eating healthier, especially compared to me, and that I needed to provide some good choices along with my tried and true way to eat when she's not around."

Kate opens the closet next to Joshua's front door and hangs her coat inside. "Yes, if I remember right, your main sources of nourishment were noodles and hot dogs, from your dorm days all the way up until you met her."

"And while I am much improved since my dorm days, noodles and hot dogs still would be my main food source if I didn't have her," Joshua admits. They both laugh as they sit down in the living room. Kate grabs her plate and takes a few pieces of fruit and begins to eat, hungry from her extended drive. "So, my friend, where did we leave off?" Joshua asks.

Kate takes a drink of hot chocolate and sets the mug down on the table. "If I remember correctly, you told me about the change from management to leadership, and I asked you what the change had to do with employee empowerment and engagement.

"I've been waiting all week to find out the answer," Kate half jokes.

Joshua nods. "All right, then. Your wait is over. However, as I mentioned last week, it's a lengthy discussion, so let's start out slow and work our way forward."

"OK," Kate says. She takes another drink of hot chocolate and holds on to the mug.

"So, first off, what do you think empowerment is?"

Kate crinkles her forehead. "Well, I thought I knew. But we've had such a hard time trying to make it work that I'm not so sure I do anymore. If I had to say, though, I think it's giving ownership, responsibility, and accountability to the people who run the processes every day." Kate looks up at her friend expectantly and shrugs.

"That sounds...pretty good," Joshua replies slowly. "Mind if I ask a few clarifying questions and we do a little administrative exercise?"

"Not at all," Kate says, open to learning more.

"OK, so you've said that it's giving ownership, responsibility, and accountability to the people who run the processes daily." Kate nods. Joshua continues, "So what I would like to know is...when you ask your employees to be empowered, what specifically do you want them to do with the process?" He pauses for a moment. "More to the point, how do you expect them to behave when they're empowered?"

"Well—" Kate starts.

"Wait. Hold on a minute," Joshua asks. He gets up and heads into the kitchen. A moment later, he comes out with a pen and notepad. "How about you write down all the things you want them to do and all the behaviors you want them to demonstrate," Joshua says as he hands her the pen and notepad. "Include all the expectations you have and the ones you've heard within your organization when others are talking about employee empowerment and engagement."

Kate nods, and Joshua sits back down as she begins to think about the conversations she's had and heard. When she's satisfied with the list, she turns the notepad over and slides it to Joshua's side of the table.

Joshua takes it and reads what she has written. After looking at it for a minute, he looks up and comments. "So, to summarize, you want them to take initiative, communicate clearly, help solve problems, and help improve the processes. And they should be positive, customer-focused, and willing to help others." Kate nods. "This is a pretty good list, and it's very similar to the ones I've received from other companies I've worked with."

"So when you ask about empowerment or employee engagement, everyone wants the same things?" Kate asks.

"There may be some small differences," Joshua tells her, "but every group closely identifies the same wants and needs when it comes to empowered or engaged employees."

"So that should make it easy," Kate says, frowning. "Why isn't it?"

"The difficulty isn't that they don't want the same things," Joshua says as he sets the notebook back down. "It's that they don't really recognize what it is they're asking for."

"What do you mean? It seems pretty straightforward. Empowered employees, right?"

"Do you remember when we defined *leadership* last week?" Joshua asks. Kate nods. "Do you remember *how* we defined it?"

Kate shakes her head. "Not clearly."

"In its simplest form, leadership is helping yourself or someone else transition from an unwanted or unneeded current state to a better future state," Joshua says.

Kate frowns again. "OK...?"

Joshua smiles. "With that definition in mind, why don't you look at the list you wrote down again and let me know what you think?" He slides the notepad back over to Kate.

Kate takes it and looks the list over again. She writes down the definition of *leadership* and begins drawing lines from the items on the list that could also be used to help people go forward, as the definition says. The lines on her forehead deepen as realization sets in. "What we want from empowered and engaged employees is the same as what we want from leaders, isn't it?"

"Yes," Joshua confirms. "When they say they want empowerment and engagement, what companies are really asking for from their employees is leadership. But we don't really know what leadership is, so..."

Kate smiles as the full realization of what Joshua is saying sets in. "Well, that explains why empowerment isn't working."

"Correct," Joshua says. "It also explains why there's so much conflict with employee engagement." Kate nods in agreement. "And now for the good news."

"There's good news?" Kate asks.

Joshua smiles. "The good news is that people are already demonstrating leadership on a daily basis. We just haven't recognized it."

"OK, stop," Kate says, holding up her hands in surrender. "You're officially killing my brain. First you say that we want leadership, but then you say we don't know what it is. Then you say that empowerment *is* leadership, which we don't have. And finally you say there are people who do it on a daily basis? How does all that work?"

Joshua laughs. "It's not as bad as it sounds. The conflict with leadership and employee engagement occurs because companies are asking for leadership, but they are looking for management, meaning they are looking for people to take the process back to the way it was. Most often, though, people are trying to improve the process by taking it forward."

Kate pauses for a few moments as she absorbs the statement. "No wonder so many of our people get frustrated with Frank and me. We're saying we want them to be empowered, which means we expect them to go forward like leaders. Then we get upset because they're doing exactly what we asked them to do."

"And because of this misunderstanding," Joshua continues, "the ideas and actions that emerged from empowerment efforts have been misinterpreted or misunderstood by managers and supervisors. For example, many times the questions that were asked during empowerment or employee-engagement efforts provided opportunities for the process owners to share information on how to improve and take the process forward, with information that had not been heard before. When this happened, some managers and supervisors felt like the employees had suddenly brought out hidden knowledge just to make them look bad."

Kate's mind drifts back to her own personal experiences as Joshua talks. Finally she says, "I understand how actions to go forward are being misinterpreted because managers and supervisors expect ideas that will take the process back to the way it was. But why would they feel that their employees are out to make them look bad? That sounds a little paranoid to me." She pauses. "Though now that I think about it, I guess I would have to admit that Frank and I have had similar experiences ourselves." She looks back up at Joshua. "Sometimes I've wondered why some of our employees seemed to suddenly become so smart."

"It's not that they suddenly become smart," Joshua corrects her. "It's that the leadership process—or what you are calling empowerment and employee engagement—allows them to demonstrate the knowledge and intelligence they already have."

"But," Kate starts, "and this is with no disrespect intended, only a few of them have an advanced education. Sure, the numbers have gone up recently, but they're still pretty low. Doesn't that kind of education play a role in the ability to lead?"

"Facts are not intelligence," Joshua tells her. "Whether one is memorizing, testing, or quoting the past, facts do not make anyone intelligent. It's the ability to see patterns and interactions and make connections that demonstrates real intelligence and brings about success. And most often this has to be grown through experience. When we allow people to see and interact with the whole and provide them with the information they need to go forward, usually they can do the rest."

"So when we gave our people the chance to understand and contribute ideas on how to take a process forward, a lot of that bottled-up knowledge just came pouring out?"

"Exactly. Empowerment, employee engagement, and leadership require that you ask the right questions to help the process go forward. Unfortunately, most of the experience of managers and supervisors hasn't been asking questions, but making statements to take the process back to where it was. But, again, when process owners were asked for their ideas, or asked the right questions in employee-engagement or empowerment meetings, they gave ideas for taking the process forward."

"Which would explain the struggles our operations manager is having," Kate says.

Joshua gestures for Kate to elaborate as he grabs a bite of his food.

"Well, not only has employee empowerment taken up time without getting the results he expects, but whenever he tries to participate and ask questions, either he doesn't know what questions to ask or he gets answers that make him look bad," Kate explains. She sighs. "So far, I'm seeing a lot of problems, but I'm not really getting a whole lot of solutions here."

"There are solutions, but first you have to understand what the real problems are."

"Which are what, again?" Kate asks, her mind starting to fog up.

"First, you need to realize that changes are occurring that are pushing us from a management focus to a leadership focus," Joshua says, pausing to take a drink of his hot chocolate. "And second, you need to

realize that when you're asking for empowerment and employee engagement, what you're really asking for is leadership."

"And you said that almost everyone is already demonstrating leadership on a daily basis," Kate finishes.

"Yes," Joshua affirms.

Kate nods, still trying to wrap her head around everything Joshua
has been telling her. "Do you really mean *everyone*?"

"I do," Joshua answers. "Leadership isn't about position. Leadership
is a matter of scope."

Kate gives a pained smile that betrays her confusion. "OK, I just got
that empowerment is leadership in disguise, and now leadership is a
matter of scope? Care to elaborate on that one?"

Joshua smiles sympathetically at Kate. "Based on your expression,
I'm thinking we should save that one for next week."

"Oh, thank God," Kate says, slumping forward. "I don't think my
head can absorb much more."

Joshua laughs. "OK then, how about we finish up our food and call it
a night? I'll tell you how leadership is a matter of scope next time."

Kate nods and sits up. She sighs with relief. "Same time next
week?"

Joshua nods. "Works for me. Why don't you take that list home
so you can remember what we talked about?" he says, pointing to the
notepad.

"Definitely," Kate says. She tears off the paper she wrote on and puts
it in her pocket.

Chapter 2 Work

Kate searches for Frank in his office and out on the floor. Finally she
finds him in the company cafeteria. She walks over to his table and sits
across from him.

Frank looks up and smiles. "Welcome back, partner. How was your
weekend?"

"It was great," Kate exclaims. "Saw Joshua Saturday, went to church with the family on Sunday, and we had dinner together Sunday evening. How was yours?"

Frank shrugs nonchalantly. "Went out in the woods and saw some deer and chipmunks. Realized I needed to get out there more often. I can definitely relax out there, and it helps me to be ready to come back and do what's gotta be done."

Kate smiles and nods in agreement, understanding how he feels. "That's great. And on that note, I have a question that I hope will help you start your week the right way."

Frank grins. "Fire away."

"Do you think empowerment or employee engagement has anything to do with leadership?" Kate asks.

"Whoa," Frank says, taken aback slightly. "Wow. Jeez, Kate, way to start off running." Kate smiles at him apologetically. "I take it this is what you and Joshua talked about this weekend?"

"Yep."

"OK, let me think." Frank is quiet for a few moments as he contemplates the question. He takes another sip of his coffee before he answers. "I don't know, Kate. All I do know is that if my people would just take the initiative and do things the way I've told them to do them, then they wouldn't make me have to always put things back to the way they were."

Kate raises her eyebrows in surprise at Frank and then bursts out laughing.

Frank smiles a little but looks confused. "OK, partner, you're not supposed to laugh at your friends—only with them. What did I miss?"

"Sorry," Kate says as she tries to calm down. "You just made me think about how hard we try and that sometimes we miss the mark by a wide margin."

"That's an apology? What does that even mean?"

Kate loses control again.

Frank grins and begins to chuckle. "This isn't making me feel any better, Kate."

Kate nods and takes a few more moments to finally calm down enough to talk. "OK, you remember when we talked about the difference between management and leadership last week?"

"Uh-huh," Frank answers, feeling more confused. He tries to figure out the connection Kate's trying to make. "Oh," he says, finally, "I think I see what you're trying to say. I was thinking like a manager again by trying to get everyone to take things back to where they were, right?" Kate nods. "Right, right. OK. But what does that have to do with empowerment?"

Kate brings out the paper that she wrote on at Joshua's and tells him what Joshua explained to her on Saturday.

"Dang it," Frank says, realizing that he agrees with Joshua's point of view. "No wonder everyone's ticked off at me. Bad enough I'm managing them instead of leading. But then I ask them to start acting empowered, and when they do, I criticize them for it." He drops his forehead against the table. "I have an idea—how about you just put me in the compactor and I start throwing rocks at the button," he mumbles in a defeated tone.

Kate puts her hand on Frank's arm reassuringly. "Frank, you're a good man. I've been your friend for a long time, and so have most of the people you work with. We know you care. You always try your hardest to help everyone, and you have for years. So it isn't for a lack of effort on your or my part, especially when it comes to empowerment and engagement. You've been trying to make it work for years, same as I have. The simple fact of the matter is that we didn't know."

Frank sighs and turns his head on its side. "OK, fine, fine. So there's hope. Blah, blah, blah." Kate smiles at the joke, and Frank grins. He sits up. "So what do you want to do about it?"

"Why don't we try treating our people like leaders and letting them help us move the process forward this week and see how it goes?" Kate offers.

Frank shrugs and downs the last of his coffee. "Sounds like an idea to me." He stands up to go to his office. "How about I meet you at your office in ten minutes and we can brainstorm how we're gonna get this done?"

Kate nods. "I'll see you there. Mind if I take twenty minutes so I can get some lunch for myself?"

Frank smiles. "So that's the real reason you came over, huh? You just wanted food, and I happened to be here."

"Yeah, well, *que sera, sera,* and all that. You know how it is."

"Well, then." Frank walks off in a huff, acting offended. Kate laughs.

After their meeting, Kate and Frank head out to work on leadership. At the end of the week, Frank stops by Kate's office and sees her sitting at her desk. "You know, Kate, maybe this leadership thing isn't for everyone."

Kate sighs, worn out from the workweek as well. "I feel the same, but what makes *you* say it?"

"I'm really struggling to see the connection between leadership and some of the levels of our company," Frank tells her as they both sit down at her desk, "especially with the individual process owner. I mean, it just doesn't seem like the expectations are the same. Maybe they should be, but I don't understand how. And that makes it really hard to know what questions I'm supposed to ask them too. I respect everyone and what they do, but it just seems too complicated."

Kate nods in agreement. "I know what you mean. I struggled all week to make the shift from management to leadership work. I get that when we're asking for employee engagement and empowerment, we're really asking for leadership, which helps put things in context, but..." She sighs. "Like you said, the closer we get to the level of the individual process owner, the harder the shift from management to leadership becomes. It just doesn't seem to make any sense when you're at that level. It's as if we're saying, 'Here's the process—make it work.'" Kate and Frank sit quietly, both trying to think of ways to ease the struggles they've been having. Finally Kate says, "Maybe I really should've have asked Joshua what he meant when he said leadership is a matter of scope. Guess I'll make sure to do that this weekend."

Frank forces a smile. "Well, that's great for the future, but what are we gonna do about the week we just had?"

"Well, at least everyone thanked us for trying," Kate points out. "And things were a little better than they have been."

"Fair enough," Frank replies. After another moment of silence, he asks, "So...ham sandwich?"

Kate frowns in confusion. "Ham sandwich?"

"Right. Would you like a ham sandwich?"

"No, Frank, I wouldn't."

"Why? You have a problem with ham sandwiches?"

Kate rolls her eyes and chuckles. "No," she says, getting up and grabbing her coat. "But would you like some coffee?"

"I thought you'd never ask," Frank says, standing up to join her. He throws an arm around Kate's shoulders. "And thanks so much for offering to buy again, partner."

Kate rolls her eyes again. "You know, it's not right to take advantage of a tired and confused friend."

"Well, since you're tired and confused, would you also like to play some Texas Hold'em?"

"Frank!" Kate yells jokingly.

Chapter 2 Home

When Kate walks through her front door, she sees that her husband, David, is sitting on the living room couch, looking upset. "Is it one of us or is it our daughter that's making you so unhappy?"

David flashes a tired smile. "Fortunately, it's neither you nor me today, but there's still time to participate."

"Uh, no, thank you," Kate says as she walks over to the couch. She sits down next to her husband. "Sounds pretty bad. Anything I can do to help?"

David sighs. "That girl is the smartest teenage girl I know, both for knowing what needs to be done and finding a way not to do it," he laments. "She's driving me crazy."

"OK, what didn't she do today?" Kate asks. "And would it help if I told you she just might get it from me?"

"It isn't that simple, Kate. And, no, it doesn't help, by the way," David says as he looks into Kate eyes, smiles a little more engagingly, and sits back. "She's seventeen now, and before we know it, she's going to be heading off to college. I don't want to tell her what to do. I want her to become the adult she says she wants to be and show me that she can do these things before she goes. She's always going on about this empowerment thing that they're telling her about at school and says she wants to be treated like an adult."

"But…?"

"But she won't do the simplest things. She doesn't do a single thing the way I tell her to, and I don't ever see her taking any initiative on her own, either. Just once I wish she would clean her room before she goes out with her friends, put her dirty clothes in the laundry the way I showed her instead of in her closet, and not give me any attitude about it."

Kate smiles sympathetically at her husband. "I'm sorry."

"Would you go up and back me up on this?" David almost pleads. "She seems to have an easier time listening to you."

"I'll go see what I can do," Kate tells him. She gets up from the couch and makes her way upstairs to Amber's room. As she reaches for the doorknob, she remembers the discussions she's had with Joshua and Frank over the past week and wonders, *Did David just ask me to help empower our daughter, or did he ask me to manage her?* She smiles. *No wonder we get so confused at work. We have the same problem right here at home.*

She takes a moment to quickly reorient her mind-set and then opens the door.

Amber looks up at as Kate walks in. She is putting the clothes from her closet into a laundry basket. "Hi, Mom. Did Dad send you with the bazooka?"

Kate smiles. "No. As cute as you are, he doesn't want to risk having to make another one. He wants me to work with the one we've got." She shuts the door behind her and joins Amber in cleaning up her clothes. "Now, before I say anything, is there anything I need to know before I get myself in trouble again with your father?"

Amber sighs in exasperation and sits down on her bed. "I don't understand what Dad wants some days. One moment he's telling me I'm mature enough to take care of my own room and my own laundry, and the next he's yelling at me for doing it my way. I get it done, but he always wants to go back to doing it his way. Sometimes I just wish he would make up his mind."

Kate smiles sympathetically at her daughter and sits down next to her.

"Got any ideas?" Amber asks.

"Today I think I should probably discuss any ideas I have with your father first," Kate says. "But I might know part of the problem."

"What? Adolescent or geriatric hormones?" Amber teases.

"Although I don't think so," Kate replies, "they both might be part of the problem, along with some genetics from your mother. But I'll deny having agreed with the geriatric hormones if you bring it up to your father."

"Bring what up?" she asks in mock innocence.

"Good daughter," Kate says and pats her on the shoulder. She and Amber both laugh. "OK. So, then, to the problem. When you talk about empowerment to Dad, what do you mean?"

Amber shrugs. "Mostly I mean that I want Dad to trust me enough that he gives me the responsibility and authority to get things done. OK, so usually I'm talking about the things that I like to do, but I suppose it also applies to cleaning my room and putting my laundry where it belongs as well. Why?"

"Do you remember last week when we talked about you being a leader?"

"Yeah, sure," Amber answers. "You wanted me to think about my future and how to get from where I am to where I want to be. And you said something about it involving asking the right questions."

Kate nods in approval. "Good memory. Well, I just learned this week that empowerment and leadership are the same thing."

Amber frowns, confused. "So why the two names? Isn't that a little confusing?"

"You have no idea," Kate says. "Welcome to the adult world, where we have it all worked out."

"Great," Amber says, rolling her eyes jokingly, "and I had such high hopes, too. So if I understand what you're trying to tell me, when I ask to be empowered, what I really am asking is to be a leader?"

"That's pretty much it, Amber."

"Then I don't understand why Dad gets so upset with me. He wants me to be a leader, and I am asking to be a leader, right? So why didn't he just ask me?"

"Probably for the same reasons I didn't. He knows that he wants you to be a leader, but he isn't quite sure how to help you get there just yet. He also doesn't know that when you ask him to be empowered, you're asking to be a leader."

"I get it." Amber sighs and then quickly shifts to a smile. "And here I thought you guys knew everything."

"We have lots of experience at managing and controlling. We're just a little slow on the leadership front at the moment."

"So, how about I show Dad a little leadership?" Amber says, looking determined.

"What do you mean?" Kate responds a little hesitantly.

"I need to get from where I am, which is in trouble, to somewhere better, which is with my friends. So what do I need to do to get from here to there?"

"Well, I guess you could start with getting your room from its current state to a better future state," Kate offers.

"I think I can easily handle that one. And pretty quickly at that. But I guess I should also be thinking about getting to a better place again in our relationship."

Kate looks at Amber with relief in her eyes. "Both sound great to me at the moment. I didn't have a bazooka to work with, so I am grateful that you want to try."

"You don't happen to have any suggestions, do you?"

"Not at the moment," Kate replies, standing up. "But how about we take a shot with your room, and I will work on getting you good questions for rebuilding the relationship bridge with your dad. Will that work?"

"It doesn't invoke as much confidence in your leadership skills as I would like," Amber teases Kate, "but if you'll help me with Dad for to-night, then I can wait for some help on the second part. Deal?"

"It's a deal."

"Thanks, Mom," Amber says.

"No problem, sweetie. That's what we moms are for," Kate says.

CHAPTER 3

Overview

IN CHAPTER 3, Joshua asks Kate to describe a few of the key skills her company expects from leaders, such as strategic thinking, decision making, and problem solving, and how they look at different levels of the company. After their discussion, Kate comes to understand how leadership is a matter of scope.

CHAPTER 3

Scope: The Differentiating Factor of Leadership
You Look a Lot Like Me
Recognizing Leadership at the Point of Use

WHEN KATE PULLS into Joshua's driveway, she sees Joshua talking with his daughter, Amy, and another car parked on the other half of the driveway, filled with what must be Amy's friends. Kate can't hear what's being said between Amy and Joshua, but Joshua's daughter is nodding enthusiastically and smiling.

Joshua waves at Kate, turns back to his daughter, hugs her, says one last thing to her, and then starts toward Kate's car as Amy heads toward her friends. Kate gets out of her car, and Amy calls to back to her father as she and her friends pull out of the driveway, "I love you, Dad, and thanks for the help. I promise to keep you up to date on my progress!"

"Bye, sweetie," Joshua calls back. "I look forward to hearing from you."

"How do you do that?" Kate asks as she and Joshua begin to walk toward the house.

"What do you mean, Kate?"

"Most of my friends at work would give their right arm to have that kind of conversation with their children, young or old."

Joshua shrugs. "It wasn't anything special. We were just talking about how her plan for her second year of college is progressing. You know— making sure she gets to a better future state."

They walk through the front door, and Kate starts to hang her coat up in the closet. Joshua continues, "She's becoming a strong leader in her own right, and in case you're wondering, there hasn't been anything that you and I have talked about that I don't use at home or work or in the community organizations I belong to, and that even includes my church."

They make their way to the living room and sit down. "But what about her age and education?" Kate asks. "Doesn't that affect the way you approach things?"

"Leadership isn't about age, education, or even position. It's a matter of scope." Joshua smiles. "Which I believe is our topic for this week, right?"

Kate puts her hand against her head. "Uh-oh, my brain cells are already starting to tense up. Frank and I tried to figure out what that meant at work this week, and, to be honest, we've had about as much fun as we can trying to help our people become empowered leaders. Somehow I don't think we were as empowering as we would have liked."

"How about I get us the plates of food that Lisa made for us." Maybe some food will help to get your head cleared up?" Joshua offers.

"Where is she, by the way? I'd like to see her sometime if I can. It's been a long time since us girls had a chance to hang out."

"She's out helping a group at the church get ready for the service tomorrow. She helps by working with the teen-leadership groups on Sundays."

Kate smiles. "No doubt passing along the same leadership wisdom you guys share here at your home," she says.

"Thank you for the compliment, Kate. We hope to be able to demonstrate or teach good leadership whether it's at work, at home, or in the community," Joshua says as he sets down two glasses of spring water and also two plates in the usual spot, one with chips and salsa and another with almonds and cheese. "Ready to begin?"

"Hold on a sec." Kate grabs some her water and some almonds and cheese. "OK, let's go."

"To begin, we need to understand that leadership takes a little time to develop," he begins to explain. "And it helps to start with knowing what the expectations are."

Kate nods. "That's where Frank and I got stuck. We seemed to know the expectations and things to ask from people at our level of the company, but we didn't know what the expectations should be at any of the other levels. I mean, they're different at every level, right?"

"You might think so, Kate," Joshua says, "but we found that it didn't matter at what level we asked the questions—inside a business, in the community, or even in homes. The expectations for leadership or empowerment were almost identical every time."

Kate frowns, still confused. "I guess the big question I have at the moment is, can we really expect everyone to be a leader?"

"The direct answer is yes," Joshua tells her, "but let's walk it through from a business perspective to get started. We said that leadership is helping ourselves or others go from an unwanted current state to a future state that better meets our wants and needs. So whether I'm an executive who needs to take the company from where it is now to where it needs to be or an individual process owner who needs to change my process from its current state to a better future state, either way I need to demonstrate leadership to achieve a better future state."

Kate's frown deepens. "Again, this is meant with no disrespect, but there seems to be so much more to be done at the executive level than at the process-owner level. Wouldn't the expectations have to be very different at the different levels?"

"Maybe some examples would help," Joshua offers.

Kate nods. "Yes, please."

"One of the key skills we look for in a CEO is the ability to think strategically. In business at a very high level, that means that the CEO needs to be able to look at where the company is today, identify and understand the trends that are occurring in the marketplace and inside the business, assess the strengths and weaknesses of the people and the organization, and provide a vision and plan to take them from where they are today to where they want or need to be for a better short- and long-term future."

"And that's at the high level?" Kate jokes.

Joshua smiles and continues. "A good CEO will take a look at these inputs, hear the status of the business and suggestions from the staff and advisors, and possibly seek advice and input from trusted mentors as well. He or she will then make a decision to go forward with a new line of products or services that will hopefully have long-term profitability and success for the company and its people." Joshua stops for a moment and takes a drink of his water, giving Kate a moment to digest what he has shared. "Now the details are a bit more complicated in each specific case," he continues, "but in general that's what strategically thinking means at the CEO level."

"Makes sense," Kate says. "So how does that relate to an individual process owner?"

"OK," Joshua says, setting his water down. "Now let's say I'm an individual process owner, whether a factory worker or a teller at a bank, and I have been running my machine or inputting data into my computer for a long time. But now the business is changing—say the product or service I was working on is not going to be needed in the future—and I recognize that my job will be going away soon. I look around my workplace and see that one of the new jobs coming in is a product or service that appears as if it's going to be wanted or needed for a long time. I think about it and decide that I have the skills to do that job, and it pays a little better, too, as it is a little more complex than what I have been doing."

Kate nods, following along with what Joshua is saying.

"So I put in my request for the job, use my seniority to bid for the job, or even get the inside track by being the first one to volunteer to help get it going, and a week or two later, I have a new job that's going to help me stay employed. It will also help develop my skills so that I am more valuable when the next opportunity comes around."

"That's a well-thought-out plan," Kate comments. She sighs. "But they still sound so different. How would a CEO think of the change for the individual contributor as strategic?"

"Well, a CEO might explain the situation by saying that the demand in the marketplace for a particular product or service is dying, that the demand for certain new products or services is going up, that the demand for those new products or services will likely exist for a while, and that aligning themselves and their skills with that market would improve the individual contributors' chances of longevity and increase their profitability as well."

"Ah," Kate nods, "now it sounds like the same thing. It's just that the CEO considers all of the processes and business and expresses it from that perspective, whereas the individual process owners focus only on the process they are working on and express it from their perspective." Kate looks at her friend for confirmation. "Am I saying that right?"

"Perfectly, Kate. Both are demonstrating strategic thinking, but as you can see in the visual"—he sets in on the table and turns it so that Kate can clearly see it—"the scope is different."

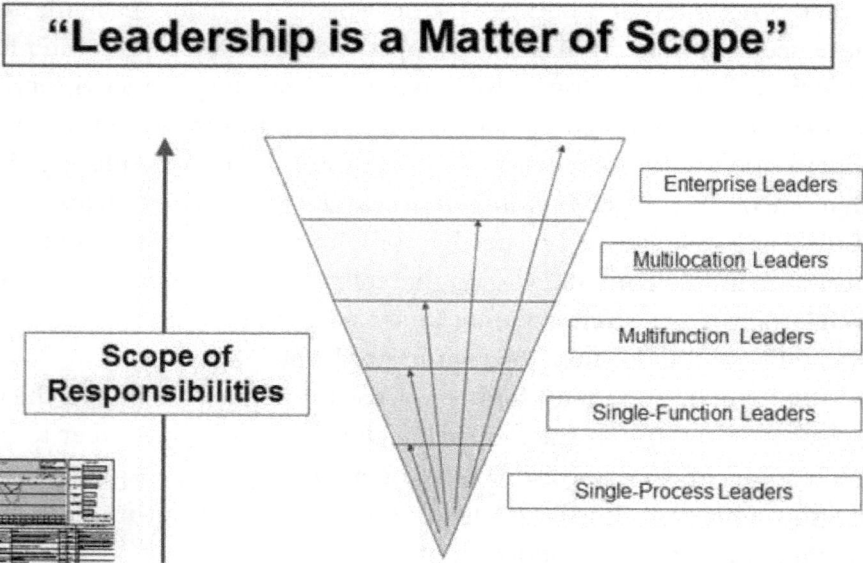

"Leadership is a Matter of Scope"

Scope of Responsibilities

Enterprise Leaders

Multilocation Leaders

Multifunction Leaders

Single-Function Leaders

Single-Process Leaders

JC Bridge Builders © 2013

Kate looks at the visual for a few moments and then sighs with relief. "OK, now this is something I can get my head around. I was starting to think that this would be so complex and different that I would never get it. Can you give me another example?" she asks.

"Sure," Joshua answers. "How about decision making and problem solving?"

Kate nods again. "That works." She sits more comfortably in her chair. "Shoot."

"As part of an executive team, if a CEO sees or becomes aware of a possible opportunity to improve business performance, to help make the best decision possible, he or she and the executive team first need to define the opportunity clearly. Then the team needs to collect and review the right information to see how customer markets, the business, and internal processes have been performing over time. and what the current customer wants and needs are. After that, they analyze the data to determine how significant the opportunity is, what the important contributors to success are, and how to best align internal capabilities to meet the new customer wants and needs. Finally, they determine how to make sure that the organization will maintain the gains that will be made through the improvement effort." Joshua pauses to see if Kate has any questions.

Kate replies after a moment. "Ok, let's see if I've got this right, only I want to focus on the problem solving side that I see a lot in our current processes." Joshua gestures for her to go ahead. "So I'm an individual process owner, and I'm having a problem with some aspect of my process that is preventing me from meeting a goal or target. "We would first have to define the problem clearly, collect our performance data to see how we have been doing over time, analyze the data to understand the significant causes that are preventing our success, determine what actions and steps we need to take to improve the process, and then figure out how to make sure that the gains we make to the process are sustained."

"Very good, Kate. You got it."

Kate pause for a moment and then asks a question. "So, if I understand it right, I could use the decision making process the same way in our business to take of advantage of opportunities that we see in our processes?"

"Your exactly right Kate, it's just a matter of scope."

"Finally," Kate says after a moment of reflection. "So we can have leadership discussions at each level of our organization," she continues. "I can't wait to get back and get started!"

"Hold on a moment, Kate. While your enthusiasm is great, it would probably be best to wait and observe leadership at the different levels for now," he cautions. "At least until we've had a chance to talk about how to create and use a leadership process."

Kate frowns. She shifts uncomfortably for a moment, impatient at the idea. "At this point, I know to trust you, Joshua," she says, "but don't I already know how to use it? You just walked me through a couple of examples of how to do it. What am I missing?"

Joshua smiles. "What questions do you plan to ask your employees when you get back?" he asks.

"Oh, right," Kate says, understanding lighting up her face. "Leadership is about asking the right questions."

"Not only asking the right questions, but also asking the right questions at the right time," Joshua explains. "Good leaders know what questions to ask first, as well as what questions to ask as time goes on, especially when making decisions or solving problems."

"Asking twenty questions randomly the way Frank and I did last week barely helped at all, and sometimes it made things a little worse."

"There is a process to leadership," Joshua tells her, "or, rather, leadership itself is a process."

She looks down in thought. "I thought it was about behaviors or attributes—things like that, you know? At least, that's what I've been taught and what everyone keeps saying."

"That's what a lot of people have been led to believe," Joshua affirms. "But it's not. Leadership is a process. Asking the right questions at the right time is what supports the process."

Kate sighs. "All right," she says, "I promise to wait a week and observe first before I go jumping in."

"Good," Joshua says with relief.

Kate laughs. "So should we meet up the same time next week?"

"Actually, would you mind waiting two weeks?" Joshua asks. "I'm out of town next weekend."

Kate laughs. "Well, then, I kind of have to, don't I?" They both stand up and make their way to the door.

"Thanks for understanding," Joshua says.

"Anyway, the extra week will give me a little more time to observe and prepare for our next discussion," Kate states as she begins to get her coat out of the closet.

"You know, if you want, I can travel your way next time," Joshua offers. "That way, you're not the only one spending gas money for our talks."

"That would be great," Kate exclaims. "I know Amber and David would love to see you. And if you want, you could bring Lisa along as well. That way we can all hang out and catch up when you and I are done."

"That sounds like a great idea," Joshua says. "How about I give you a call and we finalize the plans next week?"

"Sounds great to me, too, Joshua," Kate says. She walks out toward her car. "See you in a couple of weeks," she calls back.

Chapter 3 Work

Kate and Frank stand at the vending machine in the work cafeteria, Kate buying both of them a cup of coffee. She hands Frank his cup and starts looking over what she wants for herself.

Frank takes a sip of his coffee and sighs. "You know, we really should consider getting some sort of little café here at the company."

Kate raises her eyebrows.

"I'm serious," Frank says. "We should get a bunch of us together and go do a benchmarking trip twice a week in the mornings so that we have comparisons and present the idea to our CEO."

Kate smiles in amusement at Frank as she grabs her coffee. The two begin to make their way over to a free table.

"Do you think we could get the financing for the trips approved?" Frank asks.

"Uh, probably not, Frank," Kate tells him, playing along. "But this part of the benchmarking process is free. Cheers." She holds up her cup.

Frank rolls his eyes. "Yeah, yeah, cheers," he mumbles and meets her cup with his. He makes another face as he takes another sip of his coffee. "Seriously, we should give it a try. We work hard. We deserve some quality coffee that will keep us going."

Kate sighs. "OK, I can see that this conversation isn't going to go anywhere productive, so...how would you like to take a walk with me through the company twice a day for the next couple of weeks?"

"To look for better coffee?" Frank asks, hopeful.

"Frank," she warns.

"OK, OK." He sighs and smiles. "Is this another Joshua thing?"

Kate nods. "Remember last week how we were frustrated that we couldn't understand the different levels of leadership in the company?"

"Of course," Frank answers sarcastically, "that was such great fun. I got to feel my self-confidence take a swan dive."

Kate chuckles. "Hold onto that thought," she says. She digs around in her bag and brings out a notepad. "Here," she says, sliding it over to Frank. "I wrote these down yesterday after church. They're descriptions of what leadership looks like at the different levels. Take a look, and tell me what you think."

Frank continues to sip his coffee as he looks over the notes. His eyes widen as he gets halfway through, and soon he grabs the notepad. "Well, jeez," he says, his voice so loud it carries across the cafeteria, "this would've been helpful last week."

People look over at the two in surprise. Kate smiles sheepishly. "Sorry," she tells them. Slowly everyone goes back to their own lunches and conversations.

"So the expectations for leadership are the same no matter what level you're at, huh?"

"Yep. The more senior management roles are just larger and more complex."

"This definitely helps clear up the trouble we've been having." Frank drinks down the last of his coffee. "So you want to go through the company and confirm what Joshua told you, right?"

Kate nods. "You bet. I want to see how this plays out so I can get myself familiar with it. Still want to tag along?"

"Sure, be glad to. Can we include some benchmarking for the coffee?"

Kate smiles, finishes her coffee, and stands up and looks toward the floor. Her face grows serious, and she comments to Frank without looking up, "Maybe if we figure this out, they'll give us the coffee we're looking for. What do you think?"

Frank stands up, puts on a serious look, and turns toward the door. "Now we're talking. Let's go get 'em."

Two weeks later, Kate and Frank are sitting in Frank's office, excitedly poring over the notes and observations they made.

"Man," Frank says, "now that I know what I'm looking for, it's way easier to see the leadership that people are displaying." He rifles through and grabs one of the many interviews he transcribed. "Like June here, the purchasing manager. Said she's responsible for achieving their goals and reaching their targets. When I asked her how she did that, she told me she starts by bringing her team together and discussing how they're doing on meeting their goals and what would help them to do better. She then organizes the ideas and implements the top ones first and puts a system in place to make sure they don't lose any ground.

"And Nick," Frank continues grabbing another interview, "one of the testing technicians in the lab, said almost the same thing. He said that his job was to increase the number of tests he could run and to reduce the amount of variation that he's been getting in the results. When I asked him how he approached doing that, he said that he starts by looking over all the tests that he's running, decides which one needs to be improved the most, and asks the other technicians what they think would improve the testing. Once they decide what steps to take, they figure out how to make the improvements part of the procedures."

Frank slams the notes down on his desk enthusiastically. "Sure, the details vary a bit with each job, but there's a definite pattern here, and it matches with what you wrote down two weeks ago, Kate. I'm seeing displays of leadership practically everywhere now that I know what I'm looking for."

Kate nods. "That's what I noticed, too, Frank. I also noticed how much more alike we all really are. I've been thinking this whole time that we were all different from one another."

"Well, you are different, Kate."

Kate smiles. "Gee, thanks, Frank," she says sarcastically.

"No problem."

They both continue to look over the notes, Frank practically bouncing with energy. Kate's expression slowly darkens as a problem that's been nagging at the back of her mind begins to take over her thoughts. Frank looks up at her. "What's wrong?"

"I was just wondering how we're going to get everyone else to see this." She leans back into her chair. "Some people are very proud of their differences and probably won't want to hear that we're all equals— if not in scope, then at least in our ability to lead—and that there's leadership going on at every level of the company."

Frank sighs and puts down his paper. "Well, as usual, Kate, you're a total buzzkill."

Kate smiles apologetically. "Sorry."

Frank shrugs. "Eh, well, you're right. That job's going to be near impossible with some of the more senior managers. I've met a good number of them personally, and a few of them definitely have control and power issues." He slumps back into his chair and sighs again. "And that's not the only problem."

"What's the other problem?"

"Well, we saw a lot of people leading *some* of the time," Frank says, "but how do we get them to be leaders *all* of the time?"

Kate begins to rub the side of her head. "Good point," she says.

They both sigh and sink further into their chairs. "Well, this puts us right back where we started," Frank says. "We know the facts, but don't know how to ask the questions to help us get from where we are to where we want to be. Welcome to Leadership 101."

"Thanks for the pep talk, Frank."

"Think your friend Joshua will have any ideas? He seems to have all the answers lately."

"Or maybe the right questions?" Kate teases.

Frank sits up. "Oh, ha-ha. I'm serious, Kate."

Kate sits up and grins. "That's new."

"Well, don't knock it," Frank shoots back, "we don't know how long it'll last."

Kate laughs and then shrugs. "He probably will. He's been hinting at this asking-the-right-questions thing for weeks now."

"Well, hurry up and get him to tell you already," he orders. "I don't want to have to figure this out all on my own."

"Frank, you can barely make it through a conversation with Julie unscathed without me," Kate retorts.

"You want some coffee?" Kate groans as Frank gets up and grabs his coat. "What? I hear it helps stimulate thinking. And our benchmarking study has been looking a little thin on outside comparison."

"Way to keep focused, Frank," Kate says. She sighs, gets up, and grabs her coat, and both of them begin to make their way out of the building.

"In all seriousness, Kate—" Frank starts.

"Wow, twice in one day? Someone should call Julie."

Frank glowers at the comment. "Anyway," he continues. "I really think we're starting to get this. I've just got this feeling. It's all gonna come together."

Kate smiles and nods in agreement. "Yeah, that's what I feel, too."

Chapter 3 Home

Kate knocks on Amber's door. "Come in," Amber calls. Kate opens the door and walks in. "Uh-oh," Amber says, "am I in trouble again? 'Cause I thought I had everything covered with Dad."

Kate notices that Amber's dressed for the cold weather outside. "You're going out?"

"My friends invited me to a bonfire," Amber tells Kate.

"Did you get all the steps you need to have done to get you from here to there?"

"Well, I still have to do a load of dishes," Amber says guiltily. "But I told Dad I'd do them as soon as I got back tonight," she quickly finishes before Kate can say anything.

Kate gives her daughter a knowing smile and shakes her head. She sits down on Amber's bed. "I'll let it slide this time."

Amber hugs Kate. "Thanks, Mom. You're the greatest."

"So I keep getting told. Plus, you've been doing better on getting along with you father, and that itself is worth a free pass."

Amber laughs and returns to finishing her makeup while Kate watches. Amber notices Kate staring. "What?" she asks.

"Huh?" Kate says as her mind comes back to the present.

"You kind of have this dopey smile on your face," Amber tells Kate.

"Thanks for the compliment, daughter of mine," Kate says.

"No problem." Amber starts to put on lip gloss. "So...what's with the look?"

"I was just thinking about how much you're becoming like a leader too."

Amber frowns. *"Too?"* She closes the lid to her lip gloss and turns to Kate. "Is this about what you've been doing at work?"

"Mm-hmm. Frank and I just spent the past two weeks observing leadership throughout the company."

Amber begins to put on mascara. "Wow. That must have been fun."

Kate shrugs. "It was, actually. We discovered that everyone can be a leader at any level of the company, and many people are already doing so. It's just a matter of looking at it from the right scope or perspective. And I was just thinking that I can see now how often you've been acting like a leader."

"I have, huh? The way you and Dad act sometimes, you would think I'm not behaving like a leader at all. Sometimes I feel like you and Dad think that I'm just breaking the rules all the time."

"No, we don't think that at all, Amber, although it does seem like you try to get out of work a lot." Amber nods, conceding a little. "But maybe I just wasn't looking at what you were doing from the right perspective."

"You think maybe I was being a leader?" Amber says, turning back toward Kate.

"Well, whenever you decide that you want something, you know how to get it, right? Especially if you're asking Dad."

"Now that's not fair," Amber says, half teasing. "He says it only works half of the time."

"OK," Kate says, neither of them buying it, "let's say that's true, even though we know it's not—even though we know it works on him all of the time because you're Daddy's little girl." Amber smiles and sticks out her tongue. Kate continues, "Each time you find something you want, you think about what you will have to do to get what you're after and negotiate your plan with your family...mostly your father," Kate says pointedly, "and once you have agreement with the important people in your plan, you put that plan in action. And ta-da—you're off to a bonfire."

"Wow, am I that transparent?" Amber asks in mock innocence. Kate smiles and nods. "And every leader does this? I thought I would have to be your...uh...close to Dad's age to be able to start being a leader."

"Nice save," Kate says to her daughter.

"Don't tell Dad I said he's old," Amber jokes. "He might not let me go to the bonfire."

"Your secret's safe with me—at least until you're safely out of the house."

"Whew. Thanks. So…back to leadership?"

"Right. Anyway, yes, what you do is a form of leadership. After all, like we've been saying, leadership is about—"

"Getting from where you are to where you want or need to be," Amber finishes, rolling her eyes at the repeated phrase.

Kate smiles. "Excellent memory."

"Well, it *is* one of my more redeeming qualities," Amber says, flipping out her hair with her hand.

"So I can be expecting straight A's in the future?"

"Ha-ha," Amber says. She sits down next to Kate, finished getting ready. "So then why is everyone always commenting about me needing to become a leader? If I'm doing it most of the time, is it that they want it all the time? Don't I get to just have some fun now and then? I have plenty of work as it is. What with the play at school, getting ready for college, the SATs, homework—"

"I think they're hopeful that you'll come to know you're a leader and will use it to help yourself and others in a positive way. And it's not more work. In fact, it'll help you get a lot of your work done faster. Want me to show you?"

Amber moves to face Kate, sitting cross-legged. "Sure."

"Let's talk about college for a moment," Kate offers.

"OK," Amber says warily.

"Where would you like to be in two years?"

"On campus, getting good grades, hanging out with some of my best friends, and having a good time," Amber answers.

"Not *too* good a time."

"Mom…" Amber rolls her eyes.

"Just checking." Kate smiles. "So, then, how are you going to get from where you are to where you want to be?"

"Well, like I said, I've already signed up for the SATs, and I'm studying for them as much as I can. I've already applied to a few different colleges." Amber thinks for a moment. "I suppose I should start filling out the FAFSA form soon and contact some of the schools I've applied to and see if there's anything extra I can do to help me get in or prepare for the classes I'll be taking."

"That's very good, sweetie," Kate tells Amber. "That's exactly the kind of stuff leaders do."

"That's it?" Amber asks. "So they just figure out all this stuff so they can get what they want?"

"Or need," Kate corrects.

"Right, right. Or need." Amber smiles playfully. "Like that blue sweater at the mall because it's cold outside and I don't want to catch pneumonia and miss the rest of my senior year?"

"I think that might depend on your grades and how much you can help out financially with that purchase, my little princess," Kate says.

"OK, fine," Amber says, backing off that discussion for the moment. She sighs. "You think I can have these kinds of conversations with Dad? I mean, it seems like we're angry with each other most of the time. He thinks I'm constantly trying to get out of things, which I'm not. It's just there really is a lot going on right now. Most of the time, I'm getting home late because of everything I've been having to do lately, and I'm really just wanting to relax and hang out with my friends before I can't anymore."

"Have you told him that?"

Amber shakes her head. "I don't really think he'll listen."

"Don't you think you should? Don't you think you owe it to him to at least try?"

Amber smiles. "Try and get to a better future state, huh?"

"Exactly."

Amber sighs and gets up. "Hey, Dad," she calls as she heads out into the hallway.

"Yeah?" David calls up.

"Can we talk for a minute?"

Kate follows Amber downstairs but heads towards the kitchen to give Amber and David time alone and to make some coffee. David sees Kate and Amber coming down the stairs together and gives Kate a wary look as Amber walks up to where David is standing. "Are you two up to something?" He asks as Kate smiles and continues into the kitchen.

"No," Amber says. "Can we sit here and talk in the living room?"

David nods slowly and turns to Amber. "Sure." He sits down on the couch, and Amber sits down in a chair across from him. "What's up?" David asks.

"I just sort of wanted to apologize. I haven't been completely open with you, Dad," Amber admits.

David crosses his arms but is curious and makes a statement that sounds more like a question. "Ok, I've noticed."

"I'm sorry that it looks like I'm skipping out on chores and stuff. It's just things have been really hectic with my life lately. I'm in the play at school, which runs until five or six in the evening. Then I come home and do homework, and then I try to get some chores done. And if I have any time left, I try to talk or spend a little time with my friends. I know I'm leaving for college soon, and I just want to have some time to enjoy my senior year. I try to get everything done, but there isn't a lot of time, and my friends are only available at certain times because a lot of them have jobs. That's why I don't always get my chores done...or at least done when you want me to."

David can only blink for a few moments as his mind tries to take in what Amber has told him. "I hadn't thought about it quite like that, Amber. That's been the most straightforward thing you've said to me in a while. Did your mom put you up to this?"

Amber shrugs. "Mom asked me to talk with you, but I've been nervous to. I thought if I told you, you would think I was making more excuses. So I just negotiated."

"Well, at least I know I wasn't paranoid," David says with a little bit of a smile. "I always felt like you had a plan going on in the background, but I couldn't put it into words." He smiles broader. "Thanks for being open with me."

Amber smiles. "Mom says that what I've been doing is what leaders do, so I thought maybe it would work for us."

"She does? How so?"

"She says that being a leader's about figuring out how to get from an unwanted current state to a better future state—that you start by figuring out what it is you want to get, you gather up the information you need, then you form a plan, figure out how to implement that plan, and then make it happen."

"Really?" he says. "That simple, huh?"

Amber shrugs. "Apparently." A horn honks outside. "Oh, that's Cindy. I gotta go." She gets up and hugs David. "I promise I'll do the dishes as soon as I get back and maybe clean the downstairs bathroom tomorrow too so we're ahead in the chores for the week."

"That sounds like a great idea. Never thought I'd hear you willing to help get a head start on things here."

Amber grins and runs to the door. "See you later, Dad."

"Have a good time, honey," David says.

"I will." Amber rushes out the door and slams it shut behind her.

"Easy on the—oh, never mind." David sighs again. "One thing at a time, David. One thing at a time." Kate begins to make her way into the living room. David looks up at her as she reaches the couch where David is sitting. "Care to explain what that was about?"

"Do you have a little time?"

David shrugs. "We have until she gets back, which, knowing her, will probably be pretty late. Think you'll be able to finish by then?"

Kate nods. "I think so." She smiles. "Come on, let's go to the kitchen and get some coffee, and I'll start explaining."

"Mind if we do a load of dishes together?"

Kate looks at him in surprise. "You want to do the dishes for Amber?"

"Well, whether I like how she does it or not, she does get her work done a lot of the time," David tells Kate. "And I admit that I never really thought about how busy she is. I've been too busy looking at what she *isn't* getting done instead of what she is doing. I think I can help her out a little. You?"

Kate nods. "I think that'll be nice." They make their way to the kitchen. "I'm sorry that it's taken us so long to see all that she is doing, how much she's growing, and the leader she's becoming. I just didn't know how to see it until now."

"You know, I think you're right, but I just don't know how to know the difference sometimes," David says. "I would really like to hear what it is you've been up to lately."

Kate smiles and begins explaining as she and David make their way to the kitchen sink.

CHAPTER 4

Overview

IN CHAPTER 4, Joshua provides Kate a simple and sequential set of leadership questions that she can use at every level of her company for creating leadership, employee engagement, and performance excellence.

CHAPTER 4

The Leadership Difference
*Roads? Who Needs Roads
Where We're Going?
Managers Make Statements;
Leaders Ask Questions*

KATE WAITS FOR Joshua to get to her house. As it turns out, they have the house to themselves: Joshua's wife had previous plans for a mother-daughter shopping trip, and David and Amber, enjoying their recently renewed communications, decided to go out to a movie and then share a pizza.

This causes Kate's thoughts to drift back to the questions she is going to ask Joshua. Thus far, Joshua has been leading the conversations, with Kate asking random questions along the way, much as she has been doing at home and at work. She finally scoffs, frustrated. *Well, Kate,* she thinks to herself, *what questions do you want to ask?* She ponders for a moment and then groans, her mind drawing a blank. "Perfect," she grumbles, "I can't figure out what questions to ask about what questions I should be asking." She smiles at the irony. "Frank would get a kick out of this thought process."

There's a knock on the front door. As Kate gets up to greet Joshua, she vows to herself that she will ask better questions today. She opens up the door.

"Hey there, neighbor," Joshua says. He hugs her. "Long time no ocean."

Kate laughs. "Come on in," she tells him and shuts the door behind him.

"Wow, this place looks even more inviting than it used to," he compliments her. "Have a place for me to put this?" he asks, holding out his coat.

"You bet. I'll take care of that," she tells him and takes his coat. "You just go and find a comfortable place to sit. I put some snacks out for us on the table and some spring water. Help yourself to some chips and salsa or if you would like to risk the more healthy type of snack I put some almonds and cheese cubes out as well."

Kate walks over to the coat closet to the side of the living room. Joshua sits down on the couch. "So how did the extra week go?" he asks.

Kate sighs. She hangs up Joshua's coat, closes the closet door, walks over, and sits down on the chair across from Joshua. "Frank and I saw a lot of leadership over the two weeks, which was great, but we struggled with how to explain it to everyone and get their buy-in, so it left us with more questions than answers."

"No pun intended?"

"Oh. Ha-ha."

"Well, that's what we said we were going to talk about, right? Asking the right questions?"

"Yeah, what are the questions?" Kate asks, exasperated. "I'm learning a lot, and I'm trying to be a good leader and ask the right questions as I go along, and I want to share what I'm seeing, but I'm not feeling like much of an expert at the moment—or any moment, for that matter."

"No one does at the beginning," Joshua consoles her. "It takes time. Knowing how to get started is usually the most helpful part."

"So how do I get started?"

Joshua smiles, leans forward, and puts some almonds and cheese on his plate. He then sits up a little to get more comfortable before he begins to talk.

"You were leading me to ask that question, weren't you?" Kate asks, noting the smile on Joshua's face.

"If you think so, sure!" He laughs and starts to talk. "OK, I want to walk you through a process, or series of questions, for problem solving.

A good leadership example will help you understand a little better and help our conversation to flow a little more easily."

Kate nods. "Sounds good to me."

"OK, when you first came to my house a couple of weeks ago, what was the problem that you were focusing on?"

"Trying to figure out why employee engagement and empowerment wasn't working."

"Why?"

"Because we need to improve, and we believe we need our employees to help us to compete with other companies in the current economy."

"Has the empowerment problem been getting worse or better over time, and by how much?"

"I know it's been getting worse," Kate laments, "because we get more requests each year to empower and engage our employees, while our employees are complaining that they dislike empowerment more than ever. Though I would have to collect some data to tell you exactly how much."

"Do you know the most frequent or impactful things that are causing it not to work?"

Kate pauses to think for a moment. "Well, when we first started, I couldn't have told you. But as we've been talking, it seems that the biggest issues were that we didn't know what leadership was and that we didn't know that when we were asking our employees to be empowered, we were really asking for leadership."

"Good," Joshua says. "Do you or Frank or anyone else at work have any suggestions on how you can fix your leadership and empowerment problems?"

"Partially." Kate smiles. "Knowing the differences between management and leadership and knowing that the expectations of empowerment and leadership are the same have taken away a lot of confusion. Also, understanding that leadership is a process has helped, as we have been trying to do things more sequentially. But not knowing what questions to ask and when to ask them has prevented us from implementing a solution that works consistently."

"If you had a solution, would you know how to make sure that the problem would not come back?"

Kate's forehead crinkles as she thinks about that. "Actually, that's something that I hadn't thought about. But at a high level, if leadership is a process like you said a couple of weeks ago, I believe we can put a new leadership process in place where everyone can see and use it, and then the problems shouldn't come back."

Joshua has a smile on his face when Kate finishes. "That's a good answer for not having thought about it. He pauses for a moment. "So, then, how do you feel now about your understanding of the problem?"

Kate hesitates for a moment. Her eyebrows go up in surprise as the realization dawns on her. "Surprisingly well, actually," she answers. "Much better than I thought I did, and it's a lot clearer in my mind than I expected it to be." She looks up at Joshua. "How did you do that so smoothly? It was like the story of my problem just spilled out. It seemed pretty jumbled to me when we got started."

"One advantage of the leadership process is that it helps us to tell our story by using the right questions at the right time," Joshua tells her.

"Why would I want to tell a story?" Kate asks a little nervously. "I'm not exactly the greatest storyteller, nor do I want to be," she says, holding up her hands in concession. What she just said runs through her mind again, and she puts her hand to her head. "Ugh, I just sounded like Frank. Now I can see why he and I get along so well."

Joshua laughs. "OK, skipping the comment about you and Frank, let me explain. Telling a story means taking the facts and presenting them in a way that helps people understand why we want or need to go from our current state to a better future state, what steps we may need to take to get there, and how to sustain the gains we make so that we can continue to grow in our success."

"Ah," Kate says, letting out a breath of relief. "So I'm not writing a story on how Frank ruined Christmas or anything." She takes a deep breath and reaches for some water and a few almonds. "So explain to me what we just did and how it works."

"First, when we are focused on solving a problem, we need to know what are goals are and if our process or processes are meeting those goals," Joshua starts. "Second, we need to know whether our success rate is getting better or worse over time, and if we are not meeting our goals, the one or two significant problems that are preventing us from meeting those goals. Third, we need to ask and understand why those one or two problems are occurring. Fourth, we need to ask for and possibly help generate one or two ideas that could help to improve the process and help us achieve the future state that we want. And lastly, we need to ask for ideas on how we can make sure the solutions we just put in place will be maintained over time and continue to prevent the problem or problems from coming back."

"So we need somewhere in the vicinity of maybe ten to, oh, I don't know, sixty-five questions to make it work," Kate states with a touch of sarcasm, but really hoping for a much better answer.

"You're actually pretty close," Joshua says, nodding with approval.

"What, with sixty-five?" Kate says, feeling concerned suddenly.

"No, with ten," Joshua says. "The number is actually half of that."

"Five?" Kate asks in disbelief and with some relief. Joshua nods. "Five? That's it?" she restates, looking for confirmation.

"Sure," Joshua responds. "To help lead a fundamental conversation on solving a problem or on decision making for improving a process, five questions will work very well."

"So then where do the other questions come in?"

"Depending on the scope or complexity of the decision we need to make or the problem we need to solve, along with the type of information that we will need, we can determine which questions or how many questions we need to ask.

Kate shakes her head, blown away by Joshua's revelation. "OK, OK. That makes sense. But still—five? What are they?"

Joshua pulls out a sheet of paper from the notepad that he brought from home and lays it on the table. "As you can see from the title at the top, these are the five key leadership questions. The questions on the left address the scope of the business that executives work with on a daily basis, and on the right side of the paper the key questions represent the typical scope of business for individual process owners."

Key Leadership Questions

Executive	Individual Process Owner
What are our key customer, business, and performance metrics and are we meeting those targets and goals?	What are your key process performance measures and are any of our processes not meeting those targets and goals?
Are our metrics performing better or worse over time, and what are our best opportunities for improving customer satisfaction, profitablity, and performance?	Is the process getting better or worse over time and what do you feel are the one or two key problems preventing the process from meeting its goals?
What are the primary drivers of customer satisfaction, business profitablity, and process performance?	Why do you think these problems are occurring?
From an innovative and integrated business perspective how can customer satisfaction, profitablity, and performance be improved?	What do you suggest we do to eliminate the problems and improve the process?
What processes can we put in place to ensure performance confidence and sustainablity?	What would you suggest we do to make sure the process maintains the gains we have made?

JC Bridge Builders © 2013

Kate reflects on the questions and looks up at Joshua when she finishes. "The process flows the same, and they ask similar questions, but the questions for the individual process owner are focused more on fixing the process through problem solving and the questions for the executive are larger in scope and more focused on leveraging opportunities to improve performance through decision making. Am I right?"

"On both counts, Kate. About ninety percent of an executive's time is spent on leveraging opportunities through decision making for designing new or redesigning current, products, services, or processes to improve success. And about ninety percent of an individual contributor's time is spent on improving the current process he or she is working with through problem solving.

She grins. "I like this idea, Joshua. I can more easily see us asking the leadership questions at every level of the company. Where did you get these? I've never seen a list like this, but I wish I'd had one before now."

"You can have those if you want them," Joshua says, as he reaches for a bottle of water. "But to answer your question, many of the questions, if not most of them, come from the performance-excellence community."

"Really?" Kate asks, surprised. "I always thought that performance excellence was about some kind of quality tools or efficiency methods. You know—that type of thing. I never would have looked to them for leadership, except maybe on a project or something. So what process do they use? It looks a little familiar, but I just can't place it."

Joshua pulls out another visual aid and shows it to Kate.

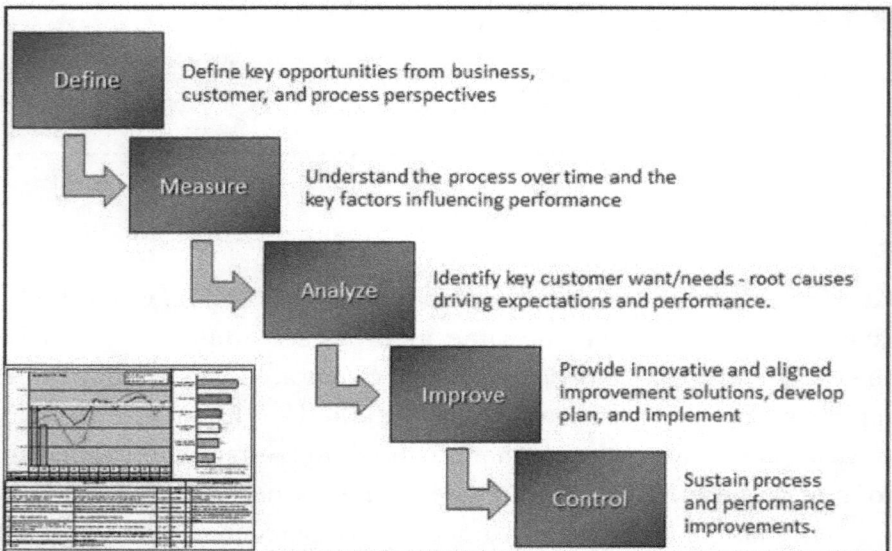

Define — Define key opportunities from business, customer, and process perspectives

Measure — Understand the process over time and the key factors influencing performance

Analyze — Identify key customer want/needs - root causes driving expectations and performance.

Improve — Provide innovative and aligned improvement solutions, develop plan, and implement

Control — Sustain process and performance improvements.

JC Bridge Builders © 2013

"The process you see here walks you through a sequence that will help you to clearly define a problem or opportunity, identify what information you need in order to understand the problem or opportunity better, analyze the information you do gather, generate ideas for fixing the problem or leveraging the opportunity, and make sure you maintain the gains you make."

Kate smiles. "Oh, right. You know I've heard you say it a thousand times by now. I should have this memorized. Is there an easy way to remember what order they're in?"

"The performance-excellence community uses an acronym for problem solving: DMAIC," Joshua says, pointing to the visual aid. "Define, measure, analyze, improve, and control. Each time they're trying to solve a problem or improve process performance, they follow this method."

"Whether they are solving a problem or helping to make a decision?" Kate asks.

"At a fundamental level, the answer is yes. Many groups have created different acronyms for the decision-making process, but it still follows the basic DMAIC sequence and objective of helping them to get from a current state to a better future state."

Kate smiles and rolls her eyes at Joshua's constant driving home of the idea of going from a current state to a future state. "You know, Joshua, the more I hear, the more it sounds like leadership," Kate comments.

"It *is* leadership, Kate. What was not always clear to leadership and even the performance-excellence community was that while they were leading efforts to improve the business, they were asking questions that were helping to develop leadership capabilities."

"Really? What capabilities do you mean?" Kate asks.

"They were helping to develop analytical problem solving and decision making by using the DMAIC process: creating interactive and engaged communications and reducing conflict by asking the right leadership questions and using the performance-excellence visuals as data repositories; providing business insights and perspectives through utilizing process and systems thinking while resolving complex or integrated process issues; encouraging project leadership and diversity through organizing and facilitating multifunctional and multilocational team efforts and meetings, developing individual and group leadership communications through storytelling during stage-gate reviews and project-completion presentations; providing individual and group leadership development and succession planning though mentoring, and coaching and change leadership capabilities by helping individuals and groups to engage in and participate in change initiatives that would take them from unwanted current states to better future states."

"I take back all the things I said about performance-excellence groups. There is a lot more going on than I thought," Kate says. But after a moment of reflection, she sits back up, looking a little perplexed. "Joshua, I get the leadership questions and the DMAIC process flow and the leadership capabilities that are being developed while the performance-excellence people are leading improvement efforts. But all that I have ever seen from them is a focus and emphasis on methods and tools. No disrespect intended," she quickly adds. "So when I think about what I have seen them do and what you are saying, I am struggling a little to bring it all together. How is it all connected?"

"I'm sure none of the performance-excellence people will take it personally, Kate. Many of them might even agree. But let's take a moment to look at how the performance-excellence community got its start and how they developed the leadership questions."

"Sure, Joshua, but you need to know that this might be a tough sell for me. I know a lot of performance-excellence people, and although many of them are very nice people and very effective at their jobs, I don't recall having any of them show me that what they do is leadership. I've been through some of the training and have a couple of certifications, but all I ever heard was about projects and tools."

"I understand, Kate. Most of the focus in the performance-excellence community *is* on the tools and methods. In the beginning they were focused on solving problems or helping help make decisions for businesses and organizations, and so the focus of the efforts was on gathering and providing good information. To create greater confidence and reduce risks in our problem solving and decision making, we need to gather the right information, which is achieved through asking the right questions at the right time during the stages of improvement, which, again, is what all good leaders do."

"What do you mean that this is what leaders do? Can you give me an example?"

"Sure. Many of us have had the experience of walking into a leadership meeting and presenting how we are doing in regards to making a decision or solving a problem to improve business performance. Once we begin presenting, good leaders will listen and then ask a question or a series of questions. Sometimes we have the information they are looking for, and sometimes we realize that we missed or forgot to collect the needed data. If we are missing the information, we go back and collect the data and then return to provide the additional information that is needed for making the best decision possible. The reason executives ask the questions is to clarify their understanding and to identify gaps and risks in our decision-making and problem-solving efforts."

"I've had that happen on both sides." Kate pauses for a moment to reflect. "Now that I think about it, sometimes I had conversations like that with a few of my teachers along the way. And occasionally it's the type of conversation I've been part of in our community organization and church-leadership meetings. So how are they connected?"

"Let me show you a visual, Kate; that may help."

"We start out on the left by asking good leadership questions that have a leadership objective in mind. Those questions align with the performance-excellence tools that are listed under the tools and then shown on the far right. The performance-excellence tools or visuals are data repositories that we use to organize and then verify agreement on our leadership discussions. Each set of questions and tools follows a sequence of steps, defining what is important and why, measuring how are we doing over time, analyzing what the key factors influencing performance are, identifying how we will improve performance, and putting changes in place that will control the process and sustain the gains that we have made."

Stage	Leadership Questions	Purpose	Method/Tool	
Define	Why do we need to change? How long will it take, and how much will it cost? How will this positively impact us?	Build Business Case with data, scope, costs, resources	Charter	
	What are we working on, and how is it connected to key objectives and strategic plans?	Verify alignment and significance of improvement initiative	Drill Down	
	How large is the project? Have we considered our customers and suppliers? What are the key inputs, outputs, and measurables?	Describe scope of project through value chain including suppliers, key inputs and outputs, requirements, key process steps, and customers	SIPOC	
	What is the process we are working on, and what are the key steps, handoffs, and performance requirements?	Understand flow of business process, key performance indicators, key inputs and outputs, and key handoff exchanges	Process Maps	
Measure	What information do we need, how much, and by when?	Focus on collecting only the key data needed	Data Collection Plan	

JC Bridge Builders © 2013

"So you're saying that the tools that we are used to seeing are just visual forms for organizing the answers to the leadership questions?"

"For the vast majority of the performance-excellence tools, the answer is yes. A few of them are only focused on providing data, instead of a visual, for gaining insight on information collected from the process, but even then it is good leadership questions that drive us to maintain positive interactions and to be able to collect the right information.

"So the performance-excellence people were asking leadership questions," Kate states.

"That's true, Kate, but over time, as the pressure increased to improve faster, the focus transitioned to completing the tools, as they provided the facts that management was used to having. Unfortunately, having a focus on the tools instead of the process of asking the right questions caused the performance-excellence community to become more and more focused on just providing information instead of understanding what information was needed and why: the process of completing the tools became the method of operation. This caused them to lose the connection they had with business leaders for solving problems and making decisions that affected performance on a day-to-day basis. Ultimately, the process of completing each of the tools to have as much data as possible became almost the only topic known and taught about performance excellence."

"I wish they knew how much leadership they had been providing—and could provide—going forward." She sighs. "But right now it seems that trying to implement performance excellence is creating as much conflict as the empowerment or leadership efforts. Why don't they just show the connections? Won't that clear it up?"

"Much of the gap in understanding performance excellence has been the result of the tool focus, but looking at the impacts that the performance-excellence methods and tools have had on management and leadership will help us to understand why there's additional confusion and conflict," Joshua tells her.

Kate hears the tone change in Joshua's voice. "I take it that you want to save that conversation for next week so I can work on the five questions?"

Joshua smiles apologetically and stands up to stretch. "It's important that I don't overwhelm you at any point during this. Otherwise some things might get lost. Plus, it's a little later than I thought; I should be heading home."

Kate nods in understanding, stands up, and walks toward the closet to get Joshua his coat. "All right, then, this week I'll work with Frank on asking the five leadership questions."

"Sounds like a good idea," Joshua says as he puts on his coat and walks toward the door. "We covered a lot today, Kate. Let me know how you and Frank do, and if you have any questions during the week, you are welcome to give me a call."

"I promise I will, Joshua. Just make sure your phone is on!" Kate says as Joshua heads down the steps and across the sidewalk to his car.

Chapter 4 Work

Kate hits SEND on her computer, the last e-mail that needed her attention this morning completed. She puts her computer on hibernate, proceeds out of her office, and hurries to see Frank a few doors down. Frank is currently drinking what Kate assumes is his first cup of coffee that morning…at least at work…she hopes.

"I have some questions for you," she says as she sits down across from Frank.

Frank raises his eyebrows in surprise, midgulp. He cuts himself off and puts down the cup. "First of all, I'm innocent. Whether I was supposed to do it or not, I'm innocent."

"Great," says Kate. "Since you're innocent, these questions will apply perfectly to you."

Frank frowns, confused. "Is that a trick answer? 'Cause if it is, I know where you keep your spare change. Otherwise, go ahead with the questions."

"By the way, you don't need any more coffee, Frank," Kate tells her friend. She leans forward. "I may already know a lot of the answers to the questions I'm going to be asking, but just follow along, OK?"

"Sure, anything for a friend who continues to supply coffee," Frank says, a little concerned about Kate's comment.

Kate smiles and moves on. "How is your department doing? In terms of your quality, cost, and delivery performance?"

Frank's frown deepens. "Quality is good," he answers warily. "Costs are…OK, but we're having trouble getting the schedule on our main product right."

"Has delivery been getting better or worse over the last month?"

Frank leans back and smiles. "Joshua?"

Kate nods. "Yeah."

Frank nods back. "OK." He thinks about the question for a moment and then replies, "Oh, it's been getting worse, especially in one area. It's only a little at a time, but it has been getting worse."

"Do your people know why?"

"Now that you mention it..." Frank sits up and thinks back to the conversations he's been having with his employees. "Mara and Tom have been saying that they know what the major problems are that are making it worse."

"Did they have any suggestions on how to fix it?"

"They said they did, but all I got was a bunch of yeses and nos when I asked," he says, frustrated.

"Did they say they knew how to make sure the problem wouldn't come back?" Kate continues, sidestepping the tangent that Frank's emotions were starting to lean toward.

"Me or the process issue?" Frank says, teasing. Kate grimaces, making it clear she is trying to stay on track. "Fine, fine..." He sighs and thinks about the conversation again. "They said they thought it would be pretty easy to make sure the issue wouldn't come back if they got a little help from our IT group."

"Would it be OK if we go talk to them now?"

"Uh, sure," Frank says. Kate gets up and heads out the door, and Frank quickly follows.

When they arrive at the work area Mara gives Kate a surprised look and a smile. Upon seeing Frank, however, her smile shifts to a scowl, and she tenses up. "Hey, Kate," she says warily as they walk up. "What brings you out to this area?"

"She wants to talk about our delivery problems," Frank tells her. "You guys still having problems?"

"Yep," she answers.

"Is it still like it was yesterday?"

"Nope," she replies flatly.

"Is it worse?" Frank asks, knowing what the answer will be.

"Yep, almost every day," she says with sarcasm.

Frank groans. "Great. See, this is what I mean. I hardly get anything from them." Frank walks a few steps away. Kate and Mara look at each other, and Mara shakes her head, clearly upset. Kate walks over to Frank. "They didn't used to be so short with me," Frank laments. "They used to be my friends."

"Mind if I try?" Kate asks.

"Sure, have at it," Frank tells her.

As they turn to walk back, Julie is standing behind them with a grin spread across her face. "Hi, guys," she says. She's looking at Frank. Kate realizes that she must have heard Frank. "Anything fun going on here?" she asks as they walk up to Mara and Tom, who are entering information into a computer.

"Just the usual conversation we have with our favorite Frankie," Mara answers with a sigh.

"Uh-oh. That explains why Kate's here," Julie says with a smile. Frank's shoulders drop in exasperation.

"Mara," Kate interjects, trying to get back on topic as quickly as possible. "Mind if I ask you a few questions about your delivery issues?"

"So long as Frankie doesn't get too close," Mara replies, giving him a glare that makes Frank start thinking about possible escape routes. "He wasn't my best friend on Friday."

Kate smiles in amusement. "So I'm gathering." Frank glowers at Kate. "So the delivery problem has been getting worse?"

"Yea," Mara says, "and I've been trying to tell everyone about it, but no one seems to want to listen." She glances pointedly at Frank.

"What have been the main problems you've seen with the delivery?"

"Is someone going to blame me when I tell them what's wrong?"

Kate smiles but maintains a serious tone. "No. We all have to live with this process, and I don't believe any of us individually designed or built it. I just want to know why the process isn't doing what it's supposed to do."

Mara nods; she knows from past experience that she can trust Kate. "OK," she says, preparing herself. "Our computer keeps adding or subtracting parts to the system when we enter data for each of the products that we make," she explains, pulling up the input screen. "I know it sounds like an excuse, since the numbers usually show up correctly at the end of the day, but that's only because we usually make inputs during the day or at the end of the shift to correct it. But with all the new products and the new computer program, it's been getting harder and harder to keep up. It happens with all of the parts, but the more runs we make and the more parts we add, the more errors there are."

Frank begins fidgeting a little. "I didn't realize it had been getting worse," he admits. "We've always had that problem, so I never thought to look at it more closely as a major source of this issue."

Tom walks around from the other side of the computer, wanting to join in the conversation. "Do you or Tom have any idea what may be the major reason for it getting worse?" Kate asks, acknowledging Tom's physical engagement.

"I've been working with this thing for months," Tom says, "and when we added the automatic adjustment to the files, it started giving us even more wrong numbers."

"Do you have any ideas about what we can do to fix it or make it better?"

Tom answers, "It looks like it might be off the same number of parts each time we run a particular part, so maybe IT just needs to adjust the program. Part of the problem might be that we just don't understand how to run the new system with so many different part numbers. It's harder to know which screen to use with the automatic adjustment. It seemed a lot easier to work with before."

"Do you have any suggestions that you're willing to share on how to fix it so the problem won't come back?"

Tom shrugs. "On the one hand, if you change the numbers in the program, it should stay that way," he tells them. "And on the other side, we could use some help understanding how to make adjustments to the new system. Worst case is we could keep track of it, and if it goes bad again, we could let you know."

Kate nods. "Tom, what you and Mara just shared was very helpful. And helping to keep track after we fix it would be great." Tom nods slowly, warily, a frown spreading across his face. "What's wrong?" Kate asks.

"Look, don't take this the wrong way," Tom says. "It sounds like a great idea on your part, too, Kate, but how do we know you'll actually get the work done? I know you personally, Kate, and I trust you as a person, but...well, it's not like we haven't heard promises like this before."

"I can understand that, Tom," Kate says. She takes a moment to think. Finally she says, "How about we keep my commitment posted out here in the open so neither of us can forget it? And if I can't get it done for some reason, I'll come and let you know personally what's going on. Would that be all right?"

Tom smiles a little and turns to Frank. "Why can't you talk like this anymore, Frankie? If you would talk nice to us again like Kate does, I might start buying you coffee like I used to."

Frank looks dejected. "Thanks, Tom," he mutters, "but I think this mud I'm drinking might do the job right now."

Tom's smile turns into a grin. "No problem, Frank. That's what friends are for, remember?"

Frank smiles a little. "Yeah, I hear you. Getting some good coffee again sounds like a great idea," Frank says, giving Kate the eye.

"Me too, old buddy," Tom says, looking at Frank's coffee with disgust. "Stop by later during break, and we'll head to the cafeteria and get you some of the better stuff. It might be just what you need to cheer you up." Tom and Mara begin to get back to their work.

"Thanks, guys, for the help," Kate says. "We're going to head back to the office for a few minutes and then head over to IT to see what ideas they have that can help us out."

Frank and Kate head toward their offices. Julie says good-bye to Tom and Mara and catches up with Frank and Kate a couple of seconds later. "You guys mind if I join you?" Julie asks.

"Actually, that would be great," Kate says. "I would love to hear your perspective on the conversation we just had."

"And I'd love to talk about it," Julie says.

Frank is the first to talk when they reach his office. "So how did that just happen?"

"I'm curious, too," Julie tells her. "It sounded a lot like what I do with my people, but you got to the solution a lot faster, and the conversation flowed very smoothly."

"I paid attention in class this weekend with my friend Joshua," Kate half jokes.

"You managed to get it written down, didn't you?" Frank asks. "You know I'm a visual guy."

"Well, I didn't get it written down," Kate says. She waits a moment for Frank to feel disappointed and then pulls the papers from the weekend out of her coat pocket. "But Joshua did give me these. Have a look." Frank leers at her; Kate smiles. As Frank and Julie look over the notes, Kate tells them about her conversation with Joshua.

"This is exactly what I've been trying to explain to Frank about asking questions," Julie says. "But I've never really had a clear idea which questions were supposed to come first, so I've been jumping around before I get all the information I need. You don't happen to have copies of these I could have, do you? And are there other questions?"

"Unfortunately I'll have to get back to you about more questions, but I can make a copy of these and get them to you today," Kate tells Julie.

Julie nods. "Thanks, that would be great. And as soon as you do get more questions, give me a call, all right?"

"Will do," Kate replies.

Julie turns to Frank. "You know, Frankie, this is the kind of stuff I was talking to you about the other day. You know, the leadership thing?"

Frank winces, thinking back to the conversation. "I remember," he says.

"Well, if this is the kind of stuff that you want me to do to become a leader, then you can count me in," she tells Frank. She stands up, stretches, and looks over at the clock. "I have to get back to my area now," she turns to Kate, "but as soon as you get a copy of this made, please stop by." She turns to leave but pauses to make one last comment to Frank. "You know, Frankie, if you start having conversations like this with the rest of us, I just might consider using some of the money I've made off of you to buy you a good coffee." She heads out the door. "Thanks, Kate," she calls back.

"You're welcome," Kate shouts out after her.

"I'm not sure how I feel about her buying me coffee with the money you gave her to give me a hard time," Frank says. "But since it's your money, I think I'll feel better about spending it."

"Right now, Frank, I would have to say that it's been worth every penny."

"Pennies? Come on, Kate. You know you had to spend more than that. I'm worth at least a nickel!" he says, smiling. He and Kate laugh a little, and Frank takes a deep breath. "On a more serious note, thanks a million for your help. Seeing Tom and Mara talk like that again and seeing Julie lighting up like that was worth it, whatever the cost."

Chapter 4 Home

When Kate gets home, she heads upstairs and finds Amber in her bedroom. "OK, Amber. What are we in bedroom prison for today?"

Amber looks up, coming out of the daze she was in. "Huh?"

"I was asking what trouble you got into with your father," Kate says.

"Nothing," Amber replies. "I just came up here so I could think a little."

"What about?" Kate says, pulling up Amber's desk chair.

Amber sighs, looking exasperated. "I don't get it, Mom. What do people want from me?"

"Do you mean at school, at home, or in the play?" Kate asks. "How's the play going, by the way?" she quickly adds.

"Good, I guess," Amber tells her. "And all of them, I guess. If it isn't my teachers, it's the director at the play or Dad or you. Every time I turn around, I keep getting told that I need to behave more like a leader. I know we've been talking a lot about it lately, but I'm still having trouble understanding it."

"Can you give me an example?" Kate asks.

"Well, like the play at school, for example," Amber says. "I was trying to help make the play better and telling the other actors what mistakes they were making so they could do better, and the director pulled me aside and told me that I really hurt some of their feelings. She asked me if I thought that since I was the most experienced one there, if a better way for me to help would be to ask questions to help them understand how to do it better instead of telling them what they're doing wrong."

"That sounds like a good idea. Is that how the director does it?"

"Yeah."

"Does it seem to help?"

Amber sits up a little, looking more interested. "Most of the time it does. Plus, I feel more like I'm an adult when I'm around her."

"You do? Why is that?" Kate asks.

"Because she doesn't criticize me—or anyone, for that matter—when we make mistakes," Amber says. "She isn't focused on what's going wrong, but on how we can improve on what we're doing. Most of the time, she just asks questions about what we are doing and asks us if we have ideas on how it could be done better." Amber leans forward, seeming to come a little more alive. "It makes us feel like we have some talent and that our ideas matter, especially when she uses our ideas and they work."

"Like what she's asking you to think about?"

Amber thinks about that for a moment. "I guess so. But I wish I knew what questions to ask. Mrs. P always seems to know. I only know how to let them know what they're doing wrong." She smiles sheepishly. "Is that something else I can try to blame on you?"

"I'm not sure I would go right to blame," Kate says, "but I think I have some questions that might help you." She goes downstairs and grabs the notes from her conversation with Joshua and shows them to Amber.

"Mind if I write on this?" Amber asks.

"Go ahead," Kate says.

Amber goes to her desk and begins writing. Kate gets up and slides the chair over to Amber so she can sit down, and she sits on Amber's bed. When Amber's finished, she turns back to Kate. "You know, it's funny. These questions sound a lot like what Mrs. P usually asks," she tells Kate.

"Really?"

Amber nods. "Uh-huh. I wrote down some of the questions I remember her asking next to the ones that lined up with the ones on here and then came up with a few of my own."

"What questions did you come up with?" Kate asks.

"What feeling or emotion are you trying to convey to the audience?" Amber starts. "Do you feel as though your delivery is getting better, or are you struggling with it more? What do you think is the biggest issue getting in the way? What changes can you think of that we can make to make it better? And when we get it right, do you have any ideas on how you can help yourself or the group do it that way every time?"

"Those are amazing, Amber," Kate says.

Amber smiles broadly and nods happily. "Maybe now I'll be able to understand how Mrs. P does it and start doing it myself."

Kate nods. "It sounds like maybe she'll be able to help you become the leader you keep hearing about. If you're interested, of course."

"I'm interested," Amber tells Kate. "Mrs. P is always helping out a lot, and if that's what being a leader's like, then I'm definitely interested."

"Want to meet up later in the week to see how things are going?" Kate asks.

Amber thinks about that for a moment and then nods. "Sounds like a good idea to me," she says. "You sure you and Mrs. P haven't been collaborating?" Amber asks, noticing how similar this conversation is to the one she had with her drama director.

"No," Kate says, chuckling. "Though it sounds like I could learn a lot from her."

Later in the week, Amber and Kate meet in the kitchen to talk. They both grab a glass of orange juice and sit down at the table. "So how is it going with the play this week?" Kate asks.

"Really great," Amber replies. "I asked Mrs. P if she would coach me, and she said yes."

"That's great, Amber."

"Yeah, it's been a blast," Amber says enthusiastically. "I was nervous at first because I didn't know what to say, but she kept encouraging me and giving me clues on what to say and when—well, what to ask, anyway. And after the first few days, things were already getting better—and easier too."

"Sounds like you're getting things figured out," Kate comments. "Your friends like you again?"

Amber nods. "Yeah. I felt that what I was doing before was wrong. I was trying to help, but I ended up just being demanding. I felt like we didn't have much time, so I just tried to help them get better faster," Amber explains. "I told them that and apologized and promised that I would try to do better in the future. They said that they knew I was trying to help and that they could see that something had changed, and they said they liked what I'm doing now much better. It feels like we're all friends again."

"That's wonderful, Amber," Kate says.

"Yeah," Amber sighs happily, "it's definitely great. Does this leadership thing work everywhere, Mom?"

"If you asked Joshua, he would say yes," Kate answers. "And based on what I'm experiencing at work and what I am seeing with you at home—and now at school—I would have to agree."

"Me too," Amber agrees. She takes a sip of orange juice. "You know, it's not so hard once somebody shows it to you," she says. "I know there's a lot more to it—more questions that need to be asked—but at least now I have a start, and things are getting better much faster than I expected."

Kate nods, thinking about all she has experienced up to this point about what Joshua has been teaching her. *She's right*, Kate thinks to herself. *It's only been a little over a month, and we've seen more improvement now than we have in years. How did things get so mixed up?*

"By the way," Amber says, interrupting Kate's thoughts, "I haven't forgotten the questions you asked me last weekend. You know, you're starting to sound an awful lot like Mrs. P. Are you sure you aren't conspiring in the background? Because I think that's illegal in most states."

Kate smiles. "I'm pretty sure," she says, "but I think we'll definitely have to meet up soon. We evil dictators do need to actually conspire every now and again."

Amber smiles. "OK, Mom, you're sounding weird again."

"Thank you very much," Kate replies. "It has taken me years to develop that skill, as I'm sure you will someday when you have children of your own."

Amber laughs. "Love you, Mom."

"Love you, too, Amber."

CHAPTER 5

Overview

IN CHAPTER 5, Kate asks Joshua why her company's performance-excellence programs meet such resistance from her managers and supervisors. Joshua provides a perspective that helps Kate understand the links between the needed transition to a leadership focus and the drive for performance excellence.

CHAPTER 5

Leadership and Performance Excellence
Don't Step on My Blue Suede Shoes!
Understanding the Overlaps
and Expectations

As KATE DRIVES toward Joshua's house, she can't stop thinking about how great a week she has had with asking the leadership questions. She and Frank both noticed how things were improving, not only with the work itself and performance, but also with work relationships.

But as much as she has seen improvements in the interactions between supervisors and employees, in the back of her mind, Kate can't help thinking about the amount of unease between her managers and the performance-excellence group.

As she pulls into Joshua's driveway, parks, and heads for the door, her thoughts gravitate toward the mistrust and fear she's seen between her group and the performance-excellence people. It isn't outright conflict, but every time both groups are in the same room, the tension becomes so thick it could be cut with a knife. She has expected many things from her managers and supervisors, but fear was not one of them.

Joshua opens the door and greets Kate. "Hi, Kate. Come on in." As Joshua takes Kate's coat and hangs it in the closet, Kate heads toward a seat.

"Did you have a good drive over?"

"The drive was good, but some of the drivers leave a little to be desired," Kate answers as she sits down. "You would think that some of them might try looking at the road while they're driving. Not to be picky,

86

but sometimes I would like the other drivers to notice that they're in a car, on the highway, with other people."

"They say they're getting closer to a solution for the new auto technologies," he tells Kate as she sits down. "It seems to waver somewhere between controlling the technologies and controlling the cars. Either one would be a good step forward. Some hot tea?"

"Yes, please."

Joshua pours each of them a cup. "Well, I hope it gets here soon. I like progress, but I prefer to be alive to see it. On a good note there are some snack cakes if you are looking for an energy rush or a veggie plate that might make you at least feel better about how you're eating!"

She grabs her cup of tea and takes a sip. "Ah, that's good. It definitely should help quiet my nerves a little. Plus I think I will go with the veggie plate. The last thing I want now is to be a little more excited about my drive over."

Joshua grabs his cup and sits back in his seat. "So possibly on a safer note, how are things going at work?"

Kate smiles. "On the one hand, Joshua, the questions are really helping a lot. Frank is getting along better with Tom and Mara, and their area is already working through problems that they had been stuck on for a long time. But on the other hand," she pauses as the memory of one of her managers interacting with a performance-excellence leader plays through her mind, "it's not going as well as I would like."

"Why is that?" Joshua asks.

"Remember last week when we talked about how the performance-excellence people were developing leadership through problem-solving and decision-making processes?"

"Sure, why do you ask?"

"After our talk last week, I watched them to see if I could pick anything up," Kate explains.

"What did you find out?"

"After really listening to our performance-excellence people interacting with our managers and supervisors, I could hear the leadership process at work in what they are trying to do," Kate starts out slowly. So you would think that the managers and supervisors would welcome the help, but…" Kate sighs. "It just seems that they're more upset than ever. In fact, as I mentioned last time we were together, their negative reactions of frustration and mistrust are not much different from the way they react to the employee-engagement group. So what's causing the conflict with the performance-excellence group? Are they connected somehow?"

"They are connected, Kate," Joshua answers.

"Could you tell me how?" she asks. "I'd also like to know why there's such pushback from the managers and supervisors, if you don't mind."

Joshua nods. "I'd be happy to help, Kate. The performance-excellence movement started almost at the same time as the need for the change from management to leadership appeared. As the demands for business drove the need for more leadership, it also drove the need for businesses to be more competitive. In response to the need for competitiveness, the performance-excellence community started offering methods and tools to help improve performance."

"Based on our earlier conversations, you would think that would fit really well with the drive of leadership," Kate interjects.

"Leadership and the performance-excellence methods *do* fit really well together," Joshua affirms. But management and performance excellence have the same type of conflicts that empowerment and leadership have with management."

"You mean management is trying to maintain the processes the way they are and performance excellence is trying to take them forward, the same way empowerment and leadership are working with people to go forward?"

"Exactly, but there's an additional conflict, which the performance-excellence methods and tools bring to the table, that adds extra confusion and complexity to the transition."

"What's that?"

"Remember when we first talked and we discussed how almost all universities and colleges were teaching management?" Joshua asks.

"I do, and I think I can remember a couple of classes about it, too," Kate answers, pausing as she thinks back to her experiences in college.

"One of the fundamental concepts taught in many business classes is that a good manager must be able to plan, lead, organize, and control."

Kate smiles. "You mean everyone knows about planning, leading, organizing, and controlling?" she asks with mock surprise. "Well, there goes my advantage."

"Did you know that your management advantages for planning, organizing, and controlling have been replaced by performance-excellence methods and tools?"

"They take away management responsibilities?" Kate asks, this time genuinely surprised by the comment. Joshua nods. "How do they do that?"

"As an example," Joshua begins, "in the area of planning, there is a performance-excellence method called visual scheduling. It uses visuals to help people decide what product or service to provide next and in what quantities. Instead of having a production supervisor or a scheduling manager doing the planning, the process owners can use the method right where they work."

"I've seen those used sometimes in certain areas of our business," Kate says. "But our managers don't like them too much, especially our scheduling manager. He says that only scheduling supervisors and managers know how to schedule and how to respond when something goes wrong."

"So what happens in those areas where they have visual scheduling when something does go wrong, Kate?"

"I've noticed that when the process owners were using visual scheduling tools and changes occurred in the schedule, they already had plans in place to deal with the changes. Like someone had already asked some questions about what to do if something went wrong."

"That's a good observation, Kate," Joshua says.

"So planning was slowly being removed from the manager's responsibilities." Kate sits back for a moment, realizing the impacts of the changes. "I just thought of them as helping us to improve our scheduling. I never thought of them as *replacing* the manager's role," she adds.

"What about with the other areas?" Kate asks while she sits forward, takes some carrots and celery, and places them on her plate.

"Well, the next area is in organizing, where we use one of the most well-known performance-excellence tools, called 5S," Joshua continues. "It provides a sequence of five steps to help process owners organize their work areas to be more efficient, effective, and safe."

"We worked a lot with 5S last year," Kate says. "It really helped keep the workplace organized once we figured out that we needed to ask the process owners for their ideas. It was completely different from before, when the managers and supervisors were making all the changes for them and telling them to make the revised process work. We could never sustain the new process and the performance-improvement gains when the process owners were just told what to do. I remember that it was really hard for the managers to let go of organizing everything, but the workplace really is more organized and productive now that the process owners have been reorganizing their own work areas." She smiles sympathetically. "But I see what you mean about the manager's skill for organizing being replaced."

"And in the area of controlling," Joshua continues, "there is a performance-excellence method called 'error and mistake proofing,' which has its focus on making sure that the process can't make any more of the errors or mistakes it did before."

"That one we've really struggled with," Kate tells Joshua. "Most often it seems like we are always rushing to put a Band-Aid on the process or fix it on the fly and keep moving. But where we have been successful at implementing error and mistake proofing, we've eliminated the need for the supervisor to come around and check on and fix the process."

"Most managers and supervisors work hard to make sure that the processes in their areas stay organized, meet the plan for the day, and see that nothing goes out of control," Joshua says.

"I agree with you there," Kate says. She frowns as she takes in all of what Joshua just said. "So the performance-excellence tools are taking the place of what managers and supervisors have been doing. I never thought about it that way before, but each of the performance-excellence methods you just talked about *does* take a part of the manager's and supervisor's responsibilities away from them." She pauses. "But I don't see why that would make them upset. If anything, it gives them more time to work on other things."

"True," Joshua says, "but the supervisors and managers can look bad in a few ways if we don't understand what's happening to their jobs and help them to know what they should be doing."

"What do you mean?"

"First, the performance-excellence methods and tools are de-signed to help people ask good questions, which, as we discussed earlier when we talked about empowerment and leadership, the supervisors and managers have not had a lot of practice doing," Joshua explains. "Second, when the performance-excellence leaders ask good questions by using the methods and tools, frequently they discover and provide information that the supervisor or manager hadn't seen or known about. Third, as the performance-excellence methods replace what managers and supervisors used to do for planning, organizing, and controlling in their areas, it makes them look like they're not needed or maybe that they weren't doing their jobs to begin with. And last, once the methods and tools replace the management responsibilities, most often the managers and supervisors didn't understand what they should be doing next."

"That's a good point," Kate says. "So what should they be working on?"

"Let me ask you," Joshua says as he lays a visual on the table. "If we've eliminated planning, organizing, and controlling, what's left that we haven't talked about?"

Change Leadership and Operational Excellence Organization

Workforce Leadership:

Plan, Lead, Organize, and Control

+

5S   Organize
Error Proofing Control
Kan Ban   Plan

JC Bridge Builders © 2013

Kate looks at the visual for a few moments, and then she lights up. "Aha, so that's where the leadership went! Since they took the management responsibilities away, all they had left was leading, which means they were left with the transition from management to leadership."

"Exactly."

"I get it," Kate says. "Either way, they were being forced to be leaders, but without any answers or, more importantly, any questions."

"You've got it, Kate." Joshua says with a big smile.

"Not too bad for an operations type of gal," Kate jokes. "I finally get the performance-excellence issues with our managers and supervisors. But when I think about performance excellence as leadership…" She pauses, formulating a question. "They weren't the only ones trying to help, were they?" she asks. "I seem to remember we had something like scorecards that came out about the same time the performance-excellence groups started. What happened to them?"

"There have been some very good leadership methods and tools that have helped create some very positive results," Joshua says. "Some of them, such as MBWA, or the Management By Walking Around process, and scorecards were, and are, good leadership methods and tools."

"I remember the MBWA efforts at our company," Kate says. "We walked around to each work area and discussed how it was performing and tried to make improvements to the processes based on what the operators told us was needed. But most of the time, it just became an arguing and blaming session since we didn't have a clear idea of what to focus on. On top of that, we debated on what was important and who was to blame for the process being broken. After a while, the process owners started to resent the MBWA process, and eventually it faded away."

"What about the scorecards?" Joshua asks. "Many businesses already use the process of tracking key performance targets or metrics and have monthly, quarterly, or some other periodic review of their key measures, like the examples on this chart," Joshua says as he places a visual with scorecards on the coffee table. "But not many of them have used the process to help develop leadership, especially at the individual contributor level, where they are trying to create employee engagement."

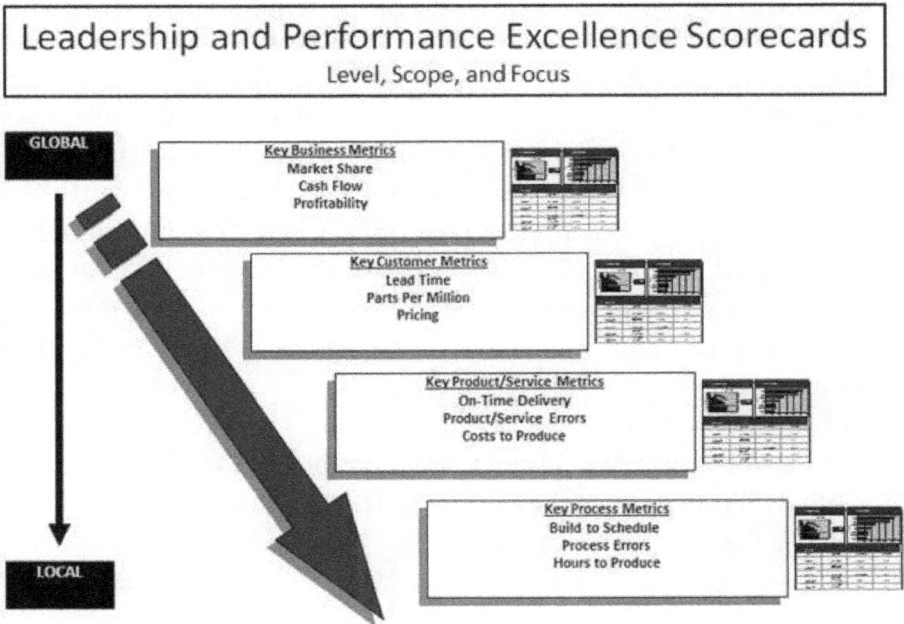

Leadership and Performance Excellence Scorecards
Level, Scope, and Focus

GLOBAL

Key Business Metrics
Market Share
Cash Flow
Profitability

Key Customer Metrics
Lead Time
Parts Per Million
Pricing

Key Product/Service Metrics
On-Time Delivery
Product/Service Errors
Costs to Produce

Key Process Metrics
Build to Schedule
Process Errors
Hours to Produce

LOCAL

JC Bridge Builders © 2013

93

"We still use scorecards," Kate tells him, looking at the diagram, "but we only use them at the higher-level management meetings. The visuals show what is important or what we need to focus on and how the process is performing over time, which is a big step forward. But there seems to be a lot of variety in how the charts are discussed, and we don't follow a consistent process on how to improve. It's been up to each manager to figure out how to make things better, and many end up managing the efforts instead of leading them."

"What do you mean?"

"Many times the manager gives an update on how they are doing and any actions they took to make it better," Kate explains. "If it isn't meeting the goal, then the manager indicates that he or she will fix it and will tell us at the next meeting what he or she did and how it worked." Kate shrugs. "There aren't a lot of questions asked, just a lot of responding by the managers about what happened."

"So how do you feel about the leadership tools?" Joshua asks pausing to take a drink of his tea and to place some broccoli and carrots on his plate.

"To be honest, Joshua, I feel the same about the leadership tools as I do about the performance-excellence tools," Kate answers. "They have their merits, but more often than not it seems that instead of bringing us together to have discussions on how to make things better and then doing it, they cause just as much conflict and confusion as the performance-excellence tools." She sighs. "I'm beginning to see how all of the tools got mixed up, whether they were from leadership or the performance-excellence communities. Is there a way we can separate them and clear up the problems?" she asks Joshua hopefully.

Joshua smiles. "What if I told you that to help clear up the problems, we need to integrate them instead of separating them?"

"What if I told you my brain just did a flip-flop?" Kate says. "How can combining them make it easier?"

"If we combine or integrate them, we can focus on developing leaders and improving the business at the same time with just one process instead of many," Joshua tells Kate.

"That sounds like it could be really complicated," Kate says.

"Actually, it simplifies things and makes the leadership process that much easier to understand and use," Joshua tells her. "How about if we take a look at the process next week, and you can tell me what you think?"

"That would be nice," Kate says. "I would like to have the chance to digest what we discussed today."

"OK, I'll see you then," Joshua says. They both stand up and stretch.

"Thanks again for meeting up with me like this," Kate says as they make their way toward the front door. "I'm enjoying our talks and learning a lot."

Joshua grabs Kate's coat out of the closet and hands it to her. "It's been nice to spend time with you, too, Kate, and to be able to share ideas again." Kate smiles and nods as she heads out to her car. "Have a safe trip home, and watch out for texting drivers," he calls out after her.

"Will do," she calls back. "Take care."

Chapter 5 Work

"I have seriously had it, Kate!" Frank bursts out as he drops down on the bench next to the vending machine. This time, it's Kate's turn to jump and look up at her friend in surprise as he breaks in on her train of thought. "Every time those performance-excellence people come into my area, I get the heebie-jeebies."

"Your mood's not contagious, is it?" Kate asks, seeing Frank's frustration, "'Cause it doesn't sound very fun."

"You know, it's like they hypnotize people or something," Frank says, ignoring Kate's joke. "They come into my work area and ask questions, and all of a sudden, they get smart and think they know more than I do."

"As opposed to…?" Kate says with a deadpan expression. She holds a coffee out in front of Frank.

"Ha-ha, Kate," he says as he takes the cup. "I'm serious. I feel like I'm being replaced, and I don't like the feeling." He takes a drink of the coffee, and they begin to make their way toward a free table. "It's bad enough that I'm supposed to be a leader—which, by the way, I'm beginning to like the idea of now that I know what's expected of me—but I swear these performance-excellence people are out to get me."

"What do you mean?" Kate asks as they sit down across from each other.

"Well, yesterday that performance-excellence guy came over and asked if he could borrow Tom and Mara for a little while to talk about the process we've been having the scheduling issues with," Frank starts explaining. "I said fine—I know I'm supposed to—but I didn't expect a lot because I'm working on it every day myself. I already know we're having data issues, and I keep working with IT and making adjustments to fix it, but the next thing I know, they're talking about a whole lot of things going on in the process that I knew nothing about."

"Like what?" Kate asks, confused and curious.

Frank sighs. "I already knew that it needed to be fixed," he says, "but some of the stuff they were talking about was brand new to me. They told him that they have their biggest issues with data errors in the afternoons, and it seems to somehow be connected with the machine heating up after it has been running for a while. So now they're replacing the machine bearings and putting them on the preventative maintenance schedule, and they're also moving the data storage to the other side of the machine so that it doesn't get so much heat on it." He takes another drink, scowling the entire time. "The last thing I need is someone coming in and making me look bad. Of course it's fast and furious around here and I can't get to everything, but why doesn't someone tell me this stuff?"

Kate frowns, again confused. "I would think you would be happy about this, Frank. This problem's been bugging you for quite a while."

"I am happy that it's getting fixed," he snaps, "but what am I supposed to do? Everywhere I turn, someone is telling me what I don't know and what I'm not doing. When are people going to show me what they want and how? They've already told me the *what* by telling me to be a leader, but that's not enough. I need to know *how*. And I want to know what those performance-excellence people are up to and why they get answers that I don't! They act a lot like the empowerment people did in the beginning." Frank pauses for a moment. "Hey, you don't think they're sharing questions or anything like that, do you?"

Kate smiles. "Funny you should ask," she says. "Joshua and I talked about this very topic over the weekend. When you're feeling a little bit better, I would be glad to at least share with you why it's happening, which is helpful by itself. And it also ties right into the leadership change we've been going through."

Frank nods. "That sounds good. You know I'll be glad to hear about it. I just needed to blow off some steam." He sighs and begins to relax a little. "I know they mean well, but it's so frustrating some days. I just don't understand it."

"Not a problem, Frank," Kate says "That's what friends are for. How about we talk after lunch today?"

"Sounds good," Frank says. He stands and prepares to head off to his office. "By the way, did Joshua tell you how to make it better?"

"He said he would tell me about a process next week that will help."

"Can't wait to see it, Kate." He drains the last of the coffee and grimaces. "How's your cappuccino fund? I think I need a double today."

"How about a soothing drink, like green tea or something?" Kate says, laughing. "You know you could use it."

Frank smiles with chagrin. "I know you're right, but I have limits, you know. How about we stick to the tried-and-true way a little longer? If this leadership process works the way I hope it will, I'll be happy to drink some green trees."

"That's *tea*, not trees," Kate corrects him, leering.

"See what I mean?" Frank says. "I need more energy to think clearer. You have some change handy?"

Kate rolls her eyes and gets up from the table. "Ever notice how I'm the one always buying the drinks?"

"Money or happiness, Kate." Frank shoots back playfully, "You can't have both."

"Right now, I don't have either," she says, half joking and half arguing.

Chapter 5 Home

"Hi, Amber. How's your day going?" Kate asks as she walks into the kitchen.

Amber grimaces. "Not as well as I'd like."

Kate, about to open the pantry, pauses and instead turns toward her daughter. "What's up?"

Amber sighs and puts down her sandwich. "I was working with my lit teacher on how to improve my grades, and he offered another method on how to improve my reading."

"Did it work?"

Amber shrugs. "It helped some," she answers honestly. "It helped me study faster and still remember what I read."

"And that's a bad thing?" Kate asks confused.

"No, it's just that it's another good thing," Amber says, sounding a little frustrated.

"What do you mean, honey? I don't understand."

"I feel like there's always so much to do," Amber laments, finally. "I mean, they want me to be a leader and do better in school at the same time. I only have so many hours in a day. How am I supposed to practice getting along better and get more work done on top of it? I'm not a machine, you know!"

"Easy, sweetie, easy. Everything's going to be all right," Kate says soothingly. She smiles. "You know, you sound like your Uncle Frank."

"Oh, great," Amber moans, "and he's the one I go to when I'm frustrated. You mean he's struggling with this, too?"

"Of course," Kate says. "We're all trying to figure out how to do better all the time and be better leaders, too."

"Maybe we should find a way to combine things instead of having to do them all separately," Amber grumbles.

The comment makes Kate pause. "You know, that's what Joshua said," she tells Amber.

Amber smiles. "I knew I liked him."

"What do you mean, sweetie?"

"Everybody else wants them separate, which just makes things confusing and hard to keep up with, don't you agree?"

Kate pauses for a moment, deep in thought. "Now that you mention it," she begins slowly, "your drama teacher seems to be doing pretty well at doing both at the same time, doesn't she?"

"What do you mean?"

"It sounds like she's been helping you become a better leader by sharing with you the right questions to ask so that your group can perform better, right?" Kate asks.

Amber thinks about that for a moment. "I never thought about it that way. She's teaching me leadership and improving us at the same time. Do you think she'd show me how she does it if I asked her?" she asks, becoming more engaged and enthused. "Because if there's a system she's been using, maybe she could teach me some of the steps. It sure would make it easier to understand and learn."

"It sounds like a really good idea to me, Amber," Kate replies. "But remember that some leaders do what they do naturally, without a system or process," she cautions. "When you ask her to show you how she does it, if she isn't sure exactly what steps she takes, ask her if she would be willing to work with you to help you understand how she decides what questions to ask. I bet she would be really happy to help you."

"I bet so, too," Amber says. She hugs Kate. "Thanks, Mom. Let me see what she says, and I'll get back to you."

"No problem, sweetie," Kate says. "By the way, when you see Uncle Frank for your weekly latte, you might want to tease him a little about how he's handling all of the leadership changes at work. You might also want to make sure to sneak him a decaf every now and then too."

Amber grins. "He's struggling that much? This might be more fun than I thought."

CHAPTER 6

Overview

IN CHAPTER 6, Joshua provides Kate with a visual process that integrates and uses executive leadership questions with a performance-excellence methodology. He explains to her that it is designed to be used by everyone at every level of leadership, whether at work, at home, or in the community.

CHAPTER 6

Building Bridges of Communication
Integration Station: I See
What You're Saying
Creating Positive Interactions
and Outcomes

As KATE PULLS into Joshua's, she notices a few yard signs stuck into the ground on either side of the driveway. Looking closely, she notices that the signs are actually charts. Kate begins to laugh. The first visual has a few different areas on it that show how many snacks Kate has had on each of her visits to Joshua's house with some suggestions on how to reduce the number of snacks she eats. The second visual, on the other side of the driveway, shows how many times Kate has chosen a healthy snack on each of her visits, plus information about goals and possible solutions for increasing the number of healthy choices she makes.

When Kate gets out of the car, she takes a couple of minutes to inspect each visual more closely before heading inside. As she opens the door, she sees Joshua setting up the last of their food. On the table is a plate with some just made chocolate chip cookies and some fresh pita bread and hummus. On a tray in the middle of the table are cups of hot chocolate "Funny, Joshua," she says, smiling. "Is this a test, she says pointing at the food choices. Or more importantly, are you trying to tell me something about my eating habits?"

"It's not a test, that's for sure. Lisa wouldn't allow it. She just wants me to make sure I provide choices. The charts are showing you an idea of what we were planning to discuss this week. The food is just handy to use as an example" he says, also smiling. "I thought it might be a good way to open up the conversation."

"Risky, but it worked," she says. She puts her coat away and sits down in her usual chair. As Joshua sits down across from her, she asks, "So, do we really need the visuals in the yard to help me reduce my snacking or increase my good food choices?"

"Putting the visuals in the yard was just for fun, but the main reason for the charts is that many people are visual learners, which means they need to *see* what we are saying to better understand."

"It seems like the pace of life is so fast now that hardly anyone has the time to read—or listen, for that matter. Maybe a picture *would* work better," Kate comments, thinking about the visuals she saw as she came in. Kate pauses, leans forward, and takes one of the chocolate chip cookies. "I can't help myself, they smell so good!"

Joshua smiles. Isn't that why we try to eat healthy most of the time and exercise so that we can enjoy the fun foods as well?"

"Yea, that's the reason! I'll eat some pita and hummus a little later." Kate says as she smiles and takes a bite of the cookie.

Joshua starts to explain the purpose of the charts. "I am sure you've heard the saying that a picture is worth a thousand words, which is true. A visual can convey much more information in a very short amount of time than a conversation, and it makes the information much easier to remember."

"So I see where a visual could be helpful. Are the visuals you had in the yard the integrated type of visuals you mentioned last week?"

"Good question," Joshua says. "The two types of visuals that we use in the performance-excellence community are designed to communicate in one direction. The first type is called visual management, and it conveys information such as the status of performance. The second type is called visual control, and it lets us know what is required or what to do next."

Kate pauses and then comments, "The ones in the yard looked like visual management, but with more information. Is that correct?"

"You're right, Kate. The visuals in the yard are two-way visual communication tools and are integrated, as we talked about last week. By design, they help to create positive interactions that lead to change, leadership development, and performance improvement."

"Does that mean it will talk back and let you know that the number of snacks I consume is fine?" she asks pointedly.

Joshua smiles broadly and leans back a little for a moment. "All right, all right. It was just humor. No need to take it so personally. Your snack consumption is not the real point anyway. Unless, of course, you think it is."

"Quite possibly," Kate admits, half joking. She takes a look at her chocolate chip cookie, smiles, and takes another bite. "So how does it work?"

"If we want leaders, Kate, we have to help people become leaders," Joshua tells her. "We need to participate in the leadership process with them to help them know how to ask the right questions at the right time, have positive interactions, and develop the perspectives they need for improving performance. This is especially true the longer we've been focusing on staying where we are or getting back to where we were. In order to make this possible, we need to create a leadership process at the point of use that will build bridges of communication."

"Having a process *would* make things easier. But what did you mean by 'the point of use'? And what are bridges of communication?"

"In general, 'point of use' means having *what* is needed *where* it is needed and *when* it is needed," Joshua explains. "In the world of business, when we provide the process of leadership to everyone where they do their work—at every level and in every environment—and they are able to use the process and demonstrate leadership where and when they need it on a consistent basis, we call that point-of-use leadership."

"I like the sound of that," Kate says, "especially the part about everyone being able to lead. So what about 'building bridges of communication'?"

"In most organizations, the largest challenge to creating a positive culture is creating an environment of positive interactions and exchanges of information that help create understanding and trust. The point-of-use leadership process creates positive two-way interactions that are focused on improving the process that is being used. Most processes are not designed by the people using them but are inherited processes or what are many times called legacy systems or processes. The positive interactions created through using the key leadership questions build bridges of communication that restore and grow positive working relationships and create sustainable success. This is achieved through focusing on not assigning blame but on understanding, improving, and sustaining the performance of the process. Once we create bridges of communication and positive interactions, we can achieve engaged leadership and performance excellence.

Kate nods in agreement. "I like the sound of that as well. To me, the leadership process is as much about communications as it is about engagement and performance. Am I missing something?"

"No, Kate, you're right on target," Joshua affirms.

"So how does the visual work?" Kate asks, turning her thoughts toward the process.

"The visual itself is typically divided into five distinct sections. First, it identifies what's important and what goals or targets we're focusing on. Second, it shows how the process is performing over time toward the goal. Third, it shows the key factors that are preventing the process from meeting its goals. Fourth, it has an area for recording the actions taken to improve the process. And fifth, or last, it can have an area for listing the ideas used to make sure that the improvements that are made are sustained over time."

"Sounds like the five questions again," Kate says.

"It is," Joshua affirms. "The five questions are integrated with the areas and data on the visual."

"Sounds like a plan. So how do the questions and chart work together?" Kate asks.

Joshua smiles and puts down his hot chocolate. "How about if I show you and explain?" he says. "It is a visual, after all." He reaches for a folder sitting on the end table next to the couch, pulls out a smaller version of the coffee chart, and lays it out on the coffee table.

Scorecards / Process Focus

D

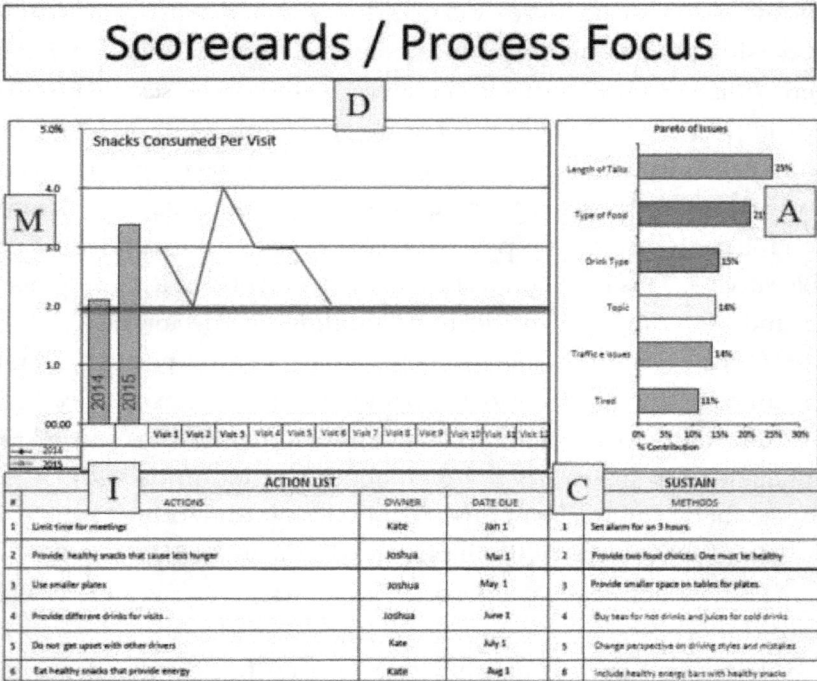

M

Snacks Consumed Per Visit

5.0%
4.0
3.0
2.0
1.0
00.00

2014 2015

Visit 1 Visit 2 Visit 3 Visit 4 Visit 5 Visit 6 Visit 7 Visit 8 Visit 9 Visit 10 Visit 11 Visit 12

2014
2015

I

Pareto of Issues

A

Length of Talks	25%
Type of Food	21%
Drink Type	15%
Topic	14%
Traffic e Issues	14%
Tired	11%

0% 5% 10% 15% 20% 25% 30%
% Contribution

ACTION LIST

C

SUSTAIN

#	ACTIONS	OWNER	DATE DUE		METHODS
1	Limit time for meetings	Kate	Jan 1	1	Set alarm for an 3 hours.
2	Provide healthy snacks that cause less hunger	Joshua	Mar 1	2	Provide two food choices. One must be healthy.
3	Use smaller plates	Joshua	May 1	3	Provide smaller space on tables for plates.
4	Provide different drinks for visits..	Joshua	June 1	4	Buy teas for hot drinks and juices for cold drinks.
5	Do not get upset with other drivers	Kate	July 1	5	Change perspective on driving styles and mistakes.
6	Eat healthy snacks that provide energy	Kate	Aug 1	6	Include healthy energy bars with healthy snacks.

JC Bridge Builders © 2013

Kate leans over to get a better look as Joshua begins to explain. "The information on the chart matches up with the five leadership questions.

"For instance, in the area where we see what is important, like how many snacks are we consuming per visit, we ask a question to define the problem: Is the process we are using preventing us from meeting any of our important goals?"

"So what was my snack goal, Mr. Joshua?" Kate asks, glowering.

"Well, that leads us to the second section. The area where we see how the process is performing over time shows that you chose to reduce the number of snacks you ate per visit to no more than two, so we ask a question to measure the various factors: are any of the steps in the process causing us to get better or worse over time?"

"Well, if I think of the steps, you invite me in, we sit down, we talk, we eat, we talk some more, we eat some more, and then I leave. So if those are the steps, then I would say that it's either the conversation or the eating.

"Sounds right. So in the third section, where the chart has an area for recording the key factors that are preventing us from meeting our goal, we ask a question to analyze the situation: what do you feel are the one or two major factors that are preventing the process we use from helping us to meet our goals?"

"To me, it's either that the conversations are getting longer or that the food is getting better and I'm eating more during each visit," Kate replies.

"Hmm…I can go along with the longer conversations and that the food is improving, but it sounds like I should let you handle the eating step," Joshua replies with a smile. "So then in the fourth section, where the chart provides a place to list our ideas and actions, we ask a question that will help us to make improvements: what ideas would you suggest we implement to improve the process?"

"Maybe we could put a limit on how long we talk. And we could still have the good food, but maybe have less of it available," Kate replies, her tone growing friendlier.

"Oh, it's *we* now, is it?" Joshua teases.

Kate laughs. Joshua continues, "Lastly, the chart provides a place to list the ideas and actions for making sure that the improvements are sustained. We ask the question that will allow us to control or sustain our progress. What would you suggest we do to make sure we maintain the gains we've made?"

"We could use an alarm so that we know how much time goes by and when our time is up. And for the food, we could use small plates and only allow ourselves to put food on our plates twice each visit. We could also make sure that one our plates is from the healthy choices section?"

"That's what we'll do then," Joshua says as they finish the example. "Sound good to you?"

"Sounds great to me, Joshua. Wow—an example *and* a solution. That was great!"

"Thanks, Kate. I'm glad you enjoyed it."

"At first I wasn't so sure, because I thought it was going to be about me. But the longer it went on, the more I realized that the questions you were asking were focusing us on the *process*, not me. That made it easy to offer information or ideas because I wasn't being blamed. I got to be part of the solution. I can see how the charts and questions are connected, and I really like how it works. Now, in the work world, how exactly would I start the conversations?"

"Good question," Joshua says.

"I'm on a roll today," Kate jokes.

Joshua smiles. "If we are walking to the work area of individual contributors to review their progress and success, we can start the discussion by asking how well the process is meeting their key goals and if it is getting better or worse over time."

Kate frowns in confusion. "If we have the charts, can't we see this on our own?"

"We can, but for at least two reasons, we want the discussions to begin with the process owners. First, we want them to help us understand why the process is the way it is, and second, we want them to be engaged in the conversation so that they can learn the process of leadership."

"I understand the leadership part—we've talked about it—but help me understand the process side."

"Process owners are the ones who take all of the inputs they're given on a daily basis and make the process work the best that it can. For example, leadership provides their people inputs such as materials or data, equipment, methods, schedules, and a place to work. They then ask them to make sure that they produce as many widgets, or provide as many services, or process as much data as they can, on time, and without any errors. Most often, though, each of the inputs the process owners have been given have built-in variations and imperfections that change while they're working. The process owners get to see how all of the interactions work together on a daily basis and over time. Because of this, they most often have much better perspectives and insights into the current problems and possibilities."

"Again, I don't understand," Kate says. "We have engineers, managers, and quality people who are pretty well educated and very knowledgeable about the processes. Why wouldn't they be better at analyzing?"

"Let me give you a different example that might help," Joshua says. "For the moment, we'll focus on people who use equipment to help them complete their daily jobs." Kate nods in agreement for Joshua to continue. "Almost everyone who owns a gas powered - push lawn mower knows that if they decide to lend their mower out, they have to share with the person they're lending it to all of the quirks that have accumulated or time and unique steps he or she will have to take in order to start the mower. When I first bought my mower and brought it home, I had to put it on choke halfway, prime it twice, pull the cord once, and it would start. But now my mower is a few years older, and so when I go to start it, I know that I first have to put the choke on full, prime it twice, and pull the cord once. Then I have to put the choke on half, prime it once, and pull the cord twice. Usually it starts on the second pull. Once it runs for fifteen seconds that way, I turn the choke off, and away I go."

"Can I borrow your mower? It sounds easier than ours." Kate says with a big smile. Then she continues, "So what you're telling me is that the person closest to the process has the most current experience with it. Even though I may have designed it, as it interacts with all of the other inputs that vary on a day-to-day basis, it may run differently from the way I thought it would, especially over time."

"Correct," Joshua says. "Once we begin to identify process problems or improvement opportunities, many times those who are closest to the process can provide the solutions that we need. About eighty-five percent of the time, those involved directly with the process know what needs to be done to make it better."

"What makes you say eighty-five percent?"

"Observations and data collected over the years from numerous employee-engagement efforts and performance-excellence efforts, including Kaizens. They have shown us that most performance solutions can be determined by observing the process as it functions and then walking through a good problem-solving or decision-making process with the process owners," Joshua replies. "The other fifteen percent, give or take a little, require a closer, more in-depth look, which usually involves the need for additional help from experts and people who work with complex interactions."

"So what you're saying is that by using this integrated visual, most process owners can solve the majority of the problems they have, and, at the same time, we can help them to develop engaged leadership." Kate pauses for a few moments and then continues. "It seems like it might be a lot of information to keep up with."

"That's a reasonable concern, especially for labor-intensive operations," Joshua says. "The good news is that there are two simple solutions. First, we could use software that is designed to work with the visual as it is." Joshua pauses and takes out a chart from his folder and places it on the coffee table. "Or, second, to achieve the process manually, we can use a modified chart like the one you see here."

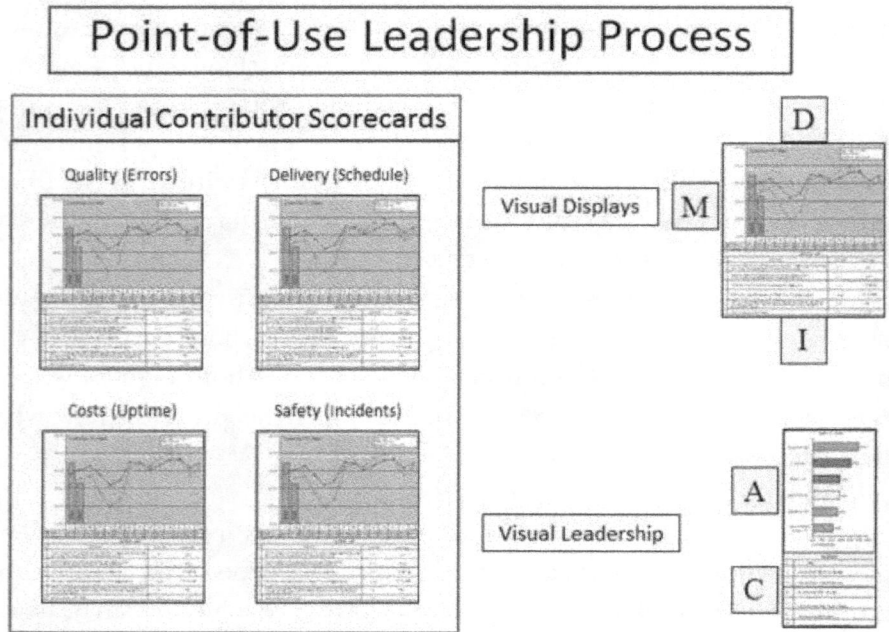

Point-of-Use Leadership Process

Individual Contributor Scorecards

Quality (Errors) — Delivery (Schedule) — Costs (Uptime) — Safety (Incidents)

Visual Displays **M** **D** **I**

Visual Leadership **A** **C**

JC Bridge Builders © 2013

"The modified version uses only the sections for identifying what we are focusing on, showing progress over time toward our goals, and recording the actions taken to improve. The other two sections—for identifying major impacts to the process and actions for sustaining the gains we have made—are covered during our leadership discussions. This provides the needed visual process and data needed for creating engaged leadership, positive interactions, and improved performance while minimizing the amount of information to update."

"I like both models, Joshua," Kate says after looking over the visuals. "They both allow us to have engaged leadership discussions that cover the four key areas of quality, cost, delivery, and safety. Plus, they allow the process owners to be engaged directly with the data through updating the charts."

Kate pauses and reflects for a moment. "It seems like if we used the process to improve performance and develop leadership at every level, then we wouldn't have such a gap identifying individuals who are ready to lead when we have open positions, right?"

"To help develop leadership bench strength on a consistent basis, we need to be aware of and leverage the opportunities and information we have from the point-of-use leadership process."

"I know we can see the performance information and how it is responding to our ideas and actions over time. But I don't feel like that is what you are talking about. What opportunities and information are you referring to?"

"As we use the process on a consistent basis, it provides us the opportunities to create observable leadership moments so that we can have meaningful real-time data for succession planning."

Is this our topic for next week?" Kate asks, knowing the answer already.

"Good insight," Joshua says, smiling. "We've covered a lot today on using visuals and the point-of-use leadership process. Saving this for next week would be perfect."

"I *see* what you're saying," Kate says, making a bad pun.

"Oh, great," Joshua says. "Give a girl a good tool, and she develops bad humor with it."

"That was good humor, and you know it. You're just jealous." Kate laughs, and the two of them begin gathering up dishes to take to the kitchen.

When they're finished cleaning up, Kate grabs her coat out of the closet and walks to the front door. "I enjoyed our conversation today. I learned a lot, and I'm looking forward to our discussion next week."

"I enjoyed today, too," Joshua says as they walk out the door and head to the car. Joshua waits as she gets in, and he shuts the door for her. Kate smiles and rolls down the window. "Thanks again, Joshua. I had a good visit, and I'll make sure not to eat any additional snacks on the way home, which should allow me to pay more attention to the other drivers!"

Joshua smiles at Kate. "Have a safe trip home," he calls as she pulls out of the driveway. She nods at him and then pulls away.

Chapter 6 Work

"Hey, Frank, have you got a little bit of time available to take a look at something with me?" Kate asks as she peeks into Frank's office.

"Is it a new coffee machine?" Frank asks hopefully. Kate rolls her eyes. "Have our studies finally started to have a positive impact?"

"No," she says. "It's a leadership visual that Joshua shared with me this weekend that I want to try in Tom and Mara's work area."

Frank smiles. "Would it be OK if we met in about an hour? I have a process issue that I need to look into right away. Then I'm free."

Kate nods. "Sounds good, Frank. I'll meet you there."

About an hour later, Frank and Kate meet up in the cafeteria. Kate buys them both a coffee. "OK, here's the visual I promised," Kate says, setting it down on the table.

Scorecards / Process Focus

D

M

Snacks Consumed Per Visit

5.0%
4.0
3.0
2.0
1.0
00.00

2014 2015

Visit 1 | Visit 2 | Visit 3 | Visit 4 | Visit 5 | Visit 6 | Visit 7 | Visit 8 | Visit 9 | Visit 10 | Visit 11 | Visit 12

2014
2015

Pareto of Issues

A

Length of Talks	25%
Type of Food	21%
Drink Type	15%
Topic	14%
Traffic e Issues	14%
Tired	11%

0% 5% 10% 15% 20% 25% 30%
% Contribution

I

C

#	ACTION LIST			#	SUSTAIN
	ACTIONS	OWNER	DATE DUE		METHODS
1	Limit time for meetings	Kate	Jan 1	1	Set alarm for an 3 hours.
2	Provide healthy snacks that cause less hunger	Joshua	Mar 1	2	Provide two food choices. One must be healthy
3	Use smaller plates	Joshua	May 1	3	Provide smaller space on tables for plates.
4	Provide different drinks for visits.	Joshua	June 1	4	Buy teas for hot drinks and juices for cold drinks
5	Do not get upset with other drivers	Kate	July 1	5	Change perspective on driving styles and mistakes
6	Eat healthy snacks that provide energy	Kate	Aug 1	6	Include healthy energy bars with healthy snacks

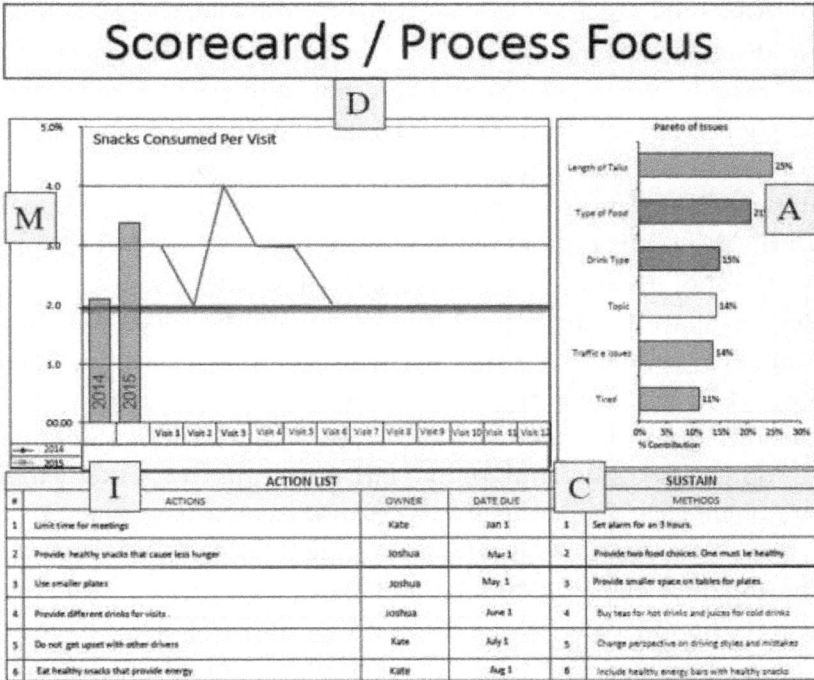

JC Bridge Builders © 2013

Frank looks it over. A mischievous smile appears on his face. "Very sexy, but your visual looks a little boxy to me," he teases. "And she looks like she eats a lot of snacks."

Kate laughs. "Ignoring how many snacks she eats, she is a very pretty chart, and she has a lot of good and important things to say to you...but you have to ask her the right questions."

"OK, but since that wasn't my strength when I was dating, how about we just treat her like a chart for now," Frank says. "Otherwise, I may get slapped by a chart, and that's not going to be very pretty at all."

"Well now, that's a visual I might be able to live with," Kate retorts with a grin. "But just to keep us on track, do you remember the questions I asked you a couple of weeks ago about what was important and whether it was getting better or worse—"

"And what was causing it to get better or worse and whether I had any ideas to make it better and stay that way?" Frank interjects.

"Exactly," Kate says. "Now, take a look at the chart and tell me if you see where and how the questions would fit in."

After a few moments, Frank points at the top of the chart confidently as he begins to explain. "Well, that's easy. What's important to our snack eater is right at the top where the *D* is. The line graph where the *M* is shows how efforts to achieve the goal are progressing over time. The bar chart and information on the right where the *A* is show what things are preventing our friendly snack eater from consistently meeting her goal. And at the bottom, where the *I* and *C* are, there are the things our hopeful snack eater is doing to improve and stay that way."

"So what do you think of our girl now? And you're really making it hard not to have you pay up on all the coffee favors," Kate says with a scowl.

"She's pretty smart, and I am referring to the chart," Frank answers, ignoring the coffee joke, "but I would like to start out slowly with her, since I can see how we could start a relationship, and I would like to do it right."

Kate frowns, sensing a shift in Frank's mentality. "Uh, Frank, I'm afraid to ask, but what do you mean?"

"If I can focus on what's important to her and learn what I can do to help her meet her goals instead of just talking at or about her, we could probably get along a lot better," Frank says, still lost in thought.

"Uh, earth to Frank," Kate says.

Frank shakes his head, coming out of his daze. "Huh?"

"What made you say that?"

Frank smiles. "I can see how the chart can help me at work, but believe it or not, I think it could help me outside of work as well," Frank tells Kate. "My girlfriend has been saying something like this to me for a couple of years, but danged if I could figure out what she meant about having a conversation. I think I see what she was saying now."

"And what's that?"

"That I need to be able to have a two-way conversation with her," Frank says. "To get to know what's important to her and how she's doing and to help her if she wants or needs it. She doesn't always want my help, but at least now I know how to carry on a conversation with her."

"I'll be. So that's what he meant," Kate muses out loud, thinking back to what Joshua said about conversations and building relationships whether at work, at home, or in the community.

"Who's he? Do I have competition already?"

Kate shakes her head. "Never mind."

"Aw, come on, don't leave me hanging like that," Frank jokes. Kate just scowls. "All right, all right," Frank says, conceding. "Since I'm not going to get any insight at the moment on possible competition, I'll just say that I really like what I see in the visual. But do you really think that using a picture is a good idea? Isn't that like an insult or something?"

"I asked the same thing when Joshua brought up the idea of using a picture—or what the performance-excellence group calls a visual," Kate says. "But he helped me see it in a different light. How about we take it along to Tom and Mara's work area? I want to talk with them about how their process improvements are coming along and share the chart with them to see what they think about it."

"Sounds good to me. Things have been getting much better between us. In fact, we have started hanging out now and then, like we used to."

"I'm glad to hear that."

"Yeah, me too. Ever since we started asking questions on how to go forward and focusing on the process instead of always stating facts about the past and looking for someone to blame, Tom and I have started to regain the friendship we had before I took this job," Frank tells Kate. "Even Mara has started talking to me again."

"Now that's a miracle, when Mara starts talking to you!" Kate says with a big smile. She pauses for a moment. "You know, I feel like I'm starting to have similar success at home."

"So Amber's been telling me during our coffee outings, although she seems to have taken a new interest in my coffee intake. Any chance you might know something about that?"

Kate smiles, "I'll plead innocence for the moment, but when we get the chance, I'd like to hear your perspective on how I'm doing with Amber."

"Definitely. We adults need to stick together," Frank says with a smile. He stands up and stretches. "So, how about we go see Tom and Mara?"

"Now that I'm thinking about this, why don't you see if Julie is available to come along too," Kate says. "I would definitely like her ideas on what she sees."

Frank nods. "I'll give her a call and see if she can meet us out there."

As Kate and Frank walk up to Tom and Mara's work area, they see Tom and Julie standing in front of the machine, talking. "Hi, Tom. Hi, Julie. How's it going?" Kate asks.

"Good, Kate," Tom answers. "What brings you back out this way? Did Frank do something wrong again?"

"No, Frank's been a good boy today," Kate says. "We still like him. I just wanted to know how the ideas for improvement have worked out. You said they were working OK about a week ago when we first made the changes."

"You know, everyone put a lot of work into the data issue, and we think it's doing better, but to be honest, we're not sure," Tom says. Mara walks around the machine to join the group.

"Do you mind me asking why?"

"Not a bit," Mara says. As long as you are still interested in hearing the good *and* the bad."

"You know I am, Mara. Even Frankie wants to hear the whole thing, right?

"You know, Kate, Mara and I are doing better here. Don't get me in trouble!"

"Frankie, you sure are a lot of fun to tease," Mara says with a big smile. "So here's the scoop," Mara says, turning toward Kate. "The good news is that I think we're doing better because I don't have to make nearly as many adjustments to the numbers, at least in the afternoons. But the bad news is that we still don't know for sure how much it's really helped. We don't have very many numbers out here, and the ones we do have most often look like gibberish to me. They want us to own the process and act like owners, but they keep us in the dark like mushrooms around here."

"Frank, do you have those numbers that I looked at with you the other day when we were talking about the impact of the improvement on this process?" Kate asks as she turns toward him. "I want to focus specifically on whether or not the solution helped the delivery numbers, since that's what started all this."

"I have them right here," Frank says, holding up the folder he's brought with him. He looks over a few of the sheets inside, writes down a couple of numbers, crunches a few numbers on his calculator, and then shows them to Tom and Mara.

Tom and Mara look over the numbers and calculations for a minute and finally look back up at Frank in sympathy. "Now I understand all your headaches," Tom says. "Can't you just show me something simple that we can talk about? This looks like those old calculus formulas we used in school that almost no one understood. Draw me a picture if you have to," he says, giving the paper back to Frank, "but please, no more of this mumbo-jumbo numbers stuff. If you want, I'll have my wife put you on the prayer chain at my church. We see a lot of miracles, you know."

"Gee, thanks, Tom," Frank says. "Just put me on the list and add it to the rest of the prayers."

Kate laughs. "I hear what you're saying, Tom, and it's a fair request." She holds out the visual Joshua showed her for walk-around discussions. "Here. I shared a visual with Frank earlier, and I would like your opinions on whether you think it could help us make this data any easier to understand and use."

"Better use a pretty visual if you're working with Frank," Tom says, taking the paper. "You know how he can be."

"Who told you?" Kate asks, smiling. As Tom and Mara look over the visual, Kate explains how it works. "Remember last time, when we talked about the process and you let me know if it was getting better or worse over time and what you thought was causing the problems, and then shared some ideas about how we could fix them to make sure they didn't come back?"

"Yeah, sure," Mara says. "When you were schooling Frankie on how to talk again," she teases.

Kate smiles. "This visual represents the leadership process I was following during our conversation," she says. "It uses information from the questions I asked."

Mara and Tom take a look at the visual. "It looks simple enough. How does it work?" Tom asks.

"We would put our goals for quality, cost, delivery, and safety performance on the chart like this second chart, and leave it at the process, recording how the process is doing on a daily basis." Kate states as she lays the second chart on the table.

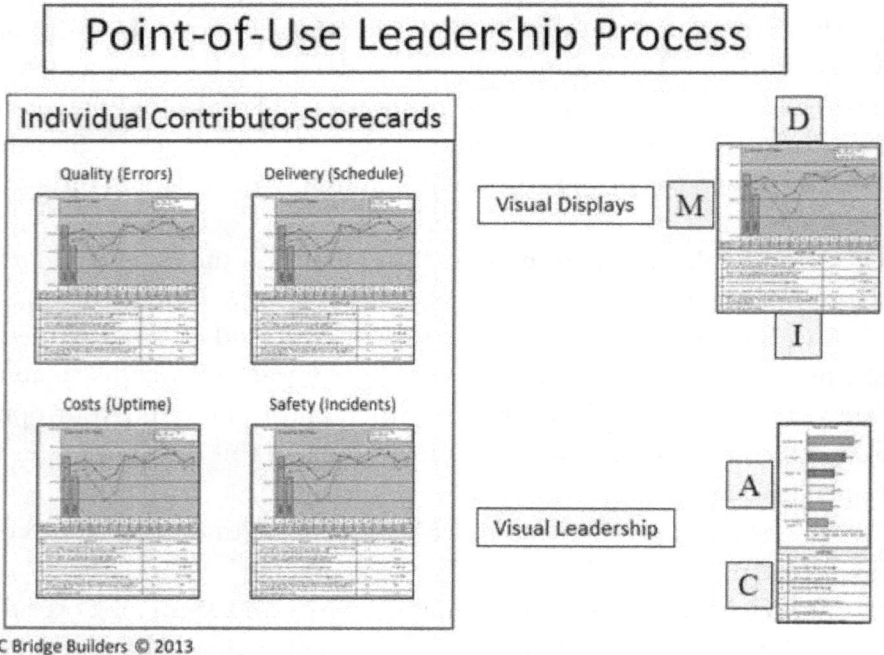

Point-of-Use Leadership Process

Individual Contributor Scorecards

Quality (Errors)

Delivery (Schedule)

Costs (Uptime)

Safety (Incidents)

Visual Displays   M

D

I

Visual Leadership

A

C

JC Bridge Builders © 2013

"Then we would talk about once a week about how it is performing over time, what might be getting in the way of meeting the goals, and what actions we would take to help improve performance. This way, you would know on a daily basis how the process is doing and how the ideas we came up with are working out."

Kate watches as Tom and Mara look over the visual a little more. She asks, "Would you be willing to try this out with Frank and me to see if it helps?"

"Looks and sounds good to me, Kate," Tom replies. "This is all Mara and I have been asking for—to let us see how we are doing. Plus, like you said, we'll get to see how well the ideas we come up with work for making this thing run better," he says, patting the machine.

"Good," Kate says. "Julie, would you be willing to stop by my office later and let me know your thoughts on this?"

"Sure, Kate," Julie says. "But I can already tell you that if you're ready to use this visual, I'm more than willing to try it in my area. We're already doing a lot of this verbally. This will help us see what we have agreed to and how it's helping. I'll stop by after my meeting if that's OK."

"That would be great, Julie. See you then."

Chapter 6 Home

Amber and Kate are in the kitchen, making some sandwiches for themselves. As Kate reaches for some lettuce, she says, "You know, Amber, I've noticed that you've been doing much better at school and here at home lately. The only struggle I see is—"

"That we talk too much?" Amber finishes.

Kate stops and looks up at Amber in surprise. "What makes you say that?"

Amber finishes making her peanut butter and jelly sandwich, scoops out some more peanut butter with the end of her knife and eats it. "Well, I love our talks," she says through the peanut butter, "but couldn't you just draw me a picture sometimes? I know you and Dad had all the time in the world when you and the dinosaurs hung out, but sometimes it's like it takes forever."

Kate sticks her tongue out at Amber, and Amber smiles smugly. She puts the lid back on the peanut butter and sets down the knife. Then she says, "Maybe it could be like the Super Bowl commercials. You know—lots of pictures but few words. They're funny, and they get to the point. Even most of the news works like that now, right?"

Kate takes that in for a moment. "Now that you mention it, I never realized how much was being communicated visually already."

"And to be honest, Mom, sometimes the words get a little jumbled up for me," Amber says. "You know I'm a visual learner. At least, that's what it showed when I took the test."

"You know, you're right, sweetie," Kate says. "I forget sometimes that not everyone learns the way I do. I do better when people tell me about things, but you've always needed a chart or something to look at before it connects." She pauses, thinking about what Joshua told her over the weekend. "Would you mind if I shared a business visual that Joshua showed me and ask you a few questions? I'd like your opinion on it."

"Will there be pop-ups, or are we working with stick figures?" Amber teases.

"Not all of us can be talented artists like you, sweetie," Kate retorts. "Some of us are talented in everything else."

"That's OK, Mom. We had a semester of interpretive art at school. I'm pretty sure I'll be able to get it."

"Gee, thanks, Amber."

"Of course."

Kate rolls her eyes and goes to get a notepad and pencil. She takes a few minutes to draw out the visual Joshua had shown her and turns to Amber when she's done. "OK, I'm ready."

"Shoot."

"What is your teacher asking you to focus on to help you become a leader?"

"She wants me to ask more questions instead of making statements when I'm offering to help."

Kate writes "questions" at the top of the chart and continues. "So, how often do you ask questions instead of making statements?"

"Well, right now I think I ask about half the time."

Kate puts "50%" in the first box and writes "current state" beside the number. "How good would you like to be?"

"I'd like to ask the right questions all the time, but I'd take nine times out of ten before the end of the play if I could have it," Amber answers.

Kate writes "90%" on the chart and puts "future state" beside it. "OK. Do you feel that you have been getting better or worse in the last several weeks?"

"Better, of course," Amber says. "But I'm still only asking questions half of the time when I have a chance."

"What do you feel is the main reason you struggle to ask questions more often?" Kate asks.

"I don't know what questions to ask when the problems come up," Amber says. "I know how to tell them what they're doing wrong, but I don't know what questions I can ask that will help them."

Kate writes Amber's statement in the top-right box. "What would you suggest to help you do better?"

"If someone would teach me or give me good questions to ask and let me know in general when to use them, I think I could do much better," Amber replies.

"How do you think you could make sure to stay at nine out of ten times?"

"Having the visual and the list together where I would be using them most often would make it easy to know what to do," Amber says. "Besides that, practice! It's easier to remember something when it works right. And because I'm a visual learner, it helps a lot when I can see that it's working."

Kate finishes putting the information in the correct areas on the chart and shows it to Amber. "Well, how do you like the visual? Is this helpful?"

Amber looks over the visual for a minute. "Actually, yeah, and it was a lot easier to talk to you, too."

"I'm glad to hear that," Kate says.

"Not to stray too far from your questions and the chart, but you've been more like a coach lately instead of a sergeant in the army," Amber says.

"Thanks…I think," Kate says, unsure where the comment was aimed.

"I don't mean that in a mean way," Amber says. "It's just that lately you ask me first and listen before you shoot. In the past it's always been ready, fire, aim. And it doesn't feel like you're upset with me much anymore, either. You still challenge me with the questions, but now the way you're asking me the questions, I feel like it's focused on how *we* can make it better instead of *you* telling me what I'm doing wrong."

"Thanks, sweetie. I love you, too," Kate says with a more relaxed smile.

Amber smiles and looks back to the chart. "So, back to the visual," she says. "Can you find me someone who has the right questions? I did ask my drama teacher about her process, and she was happy to sit with me and give me some pointers. But she said that she really doesn't know if she has a process that she follows all the time for asking questions. She said she just learned to do it by watching others and using trial and error. She said that it took a long time to learn and to get it right."

"Remember the five questions I shared with you that I got from Joshua and how we compared them with what your teacher was doing?"

"Sure, that was really helpful for me with the play."

"Well, the questions line up with the different areas on the chart," Kate states.

"OK, I am a Missouri daughter. Show me."

Kate goes through the chart with Amber and explains how each of the questions works with information shown. When she's done, she asks Amber, "So, does that make sense?"

"You bet. Someone finally took my idea and put everything together in one place. That makes it a heck of a lot easier to understand. Plus, I get a process I can see and follow. Why don't you guys do this type of thing more often?"

"We're working on it, sweetie. By the way, thanks for trying it out with me."

"Uh…you're welcome?" Amber says, still a little lost. "Will there be cash involved in this practice session?" she asks, smiling.

"Unfortunately, no. There is no cash involved. But I will make a chart with a list of the questions on it that you can use for the play. I think it'll be a good starting place to help you ask leadership questions more often and at the right time."

Amber nods in agreement. "Thanks for doing this with me, Mom. And, more important, thanks for listening and sharing a conversation with me. It really is getting more fun to talk with you, even if it was mostly guided by a stick-figure drawing," she says, gesturing to the chart and smiling.

"I'll take whatever praise I can get," Kate says. "And I'm glad to listen and share a conversation with you anytime you want."

"Thanks, Mom," Amber says as she picks up her plate and stands up. "If you don't mind, I'm gonna go eat in my room and call a couple of friends who sent me messages while we were talking. Who knows— maybe I can use this to be better at listening and being a friend to them as well."

"Not a problem, Amber, and I hope it helps. I love you."

"Love you, too, Mom," Amber says as she heads out of the kitchen.

Kate stares after her daughter and smiles to herself. *Well, I wish I had done this years ago, but I'm very grateful that I didn't miss it all.*

CHAPTER 7

Overview

IN CHAPTER 7, Joshua asks Kate how she and her organization identify, coach, and mentor their next leaders. Joshua shares a method with Kate that is within the point-of-use leadership process that allows leaders and organizations to create observable leadership moments for leveraging real-time and meaningful data for succession planning.

CHAPTER 7

Coaching and Mentoring
Gimme a Chance, Coach!
Creating and Leveraging Observable
Leadership Moments

"Hɪ, Kᴀᴛᴇ. Dɪᴅ you have a good drive over?" Joshua asks as Kate puts her coat in the closet.

"Yes and no," she replies. "No problems on the road, so that was good. The bad part was that I tried to think about what we're supposed to discuss this week, but I couldn't stop thinking about Frank and preparing him for the future," Kate says as she sits down in her usual chair.

"Does he know he's on his way out?" Joshua jokes as he heads towards the kitchen.

Kate laughs. "Of course he does. He just thinks it's for dinner and coffee again."

"I predict one of you will eventually go broke trying to feed the other," Joshua calls from the kitchen. He comes back out with two iced cappuccinos, chocolate covered pretzels, and some cups with yogurt inside and granola sprinkled on the top. He hands one of the cappuccinos to Kate, and sits down on the couch.

"You're just jealous because you have to watch what you eat and we don't," Kate teases.

Joshua laughs. "Well, aside from Frank's impending Last Supper and your lack of food sympathy for me, how are you preparing Frank for the future?"

Kate takes a sip from her iced cappuccino and takes one of the cups of yogurt. "Being serious, he's doing really well. I've talked to him a couple of times about how I think he is ready to move on to the next level of leadership. Since then, I've been looking for opportunities to watch him in action."

"How often have you been able to see him demonstrating leadership?"

Kate sighs. "Unfortunately, a lot less than I ever thought I would," she says. "It isn't that he's not working a lot, but when I went to make a list of the times I actually saw him demonstrating leadership since he came to my department, I couldn't come up with more than a couple events." She sighs again, this time with a little more frustration. "It's like this every year when they ask us to do succession planning. All of us sit around and try to think of when we saw someone demonstrating leadership—or what we used to think leadership was."

"If you don't have a lot of examples, how do you make your decisions?" Joshua asks.

"Usually someone will suggest a name and then give their reasons why they believe this person should be the next leader," Kate tells him.

"Do they provide specific examples of the person leading?"

"They usually give an example of a significant projects or work areas that the person was in charge of that turned out well," Kate says, "and if no one objects, we usually approve the candidate for the position."

"Do they talk about the how they interact with people?" Joshua asks.

"Sometimes they ask if the people who have interacted with the candidates or have worked with them would follow them. Of course, most often the knee-jerk reaction is to say yes. Otherwise they wouldn't have recommended them."

"What do they do if there's a complaint from the people on how the project or area was led?" Joshua asks, then takes a drink of his cappuccino and grabs a couple of chocolate covered pretzels.

"Generally, there aren't complaints that are considered. If the goals were accomplished, then they feel like the complaints are just as valuable as complaints that come from people working with the processes. So objections are seldom presented or listened to. In the end, it feels more like the approval is based on someone knowing the candidates and believing that they can lead. Most often, we end up with more of the same, which is another manager."

"How do the people who are trying to get promoted feel about the succession-planning process?" Joshua asks.

"They feel just as uncomfortable as we do with the process, but for different reasons," Kate answers. "Every time we mention succession planning, people start complaining that they never get the chance to show what good leaders they are or can be. On top of that, they feel that we pick the wrong person most of the time, which doesn't make things any better."

"Do the employees who are trying to get into leadership feel that they have demonstrated leadership?" Joshua asks.

"They tell us that they do, but most of the time no one is around to see it," Kate laments. She smiles. "You know, it's like that analogy about a tree falling in the forest: if a person leads in the organization and no one's around to see it, did it really happen? It's gotten to the point where many of our potential leaders quit trying to show that they can lead or even express any interest because they feel like they will never get a chance to show what they can do."

"OK, so why do they feel that the wrong person is chosen?"

"When we ask, the comment we usually get is that we pick the ones who know the process best, but that they don't really know how to work with people very well," Kate says. "The employees say they want to work with them, but trying to do so gets so aggravating that after just a short time, they go back to just doing what they are told because they would rather avoid the conflict."

Joshua smiles sympathetically at Kate. "Many organizations feel and behave this way with succession planning," he tells her. "When they come together to decide who might be ready to move forward in leadership, they struggle to provide enough of the right evidence or examples to make an informed decision."

"So what does it look like when it's done right?"

"The best scenario or outcome would be being able to say that on several occasions we saw Frank providing leadership by having very positive and productive conversations with his group or project team. And that those conversations resulted in the team taking positive actions and having a positive impact on both process and organizational performance."

"The second part sounds like the type of experiences Frank and I have been having with the point-of-use leadership process," Kate says. "So can it help us with our succession planning?"

"It can, if you choose to use the succession-planning data that it provides."

"How do we do that?" Kate asks. "Is it separate, or do we have to arrange it?"

"It's not separate," Joshua says. "Each time we have process-performance discussions and use the point-of-use leadership process, we are creating observable leadership moments. We just need to recognize that it's occurring and leverage the information that's already there."

"Really," Kate says surprised. "So how does it work?"

"Each time we're interacting in the process, we get a chance to observe how people become engaged in the process through asking questions or providing insights and ideas to help improve performance," Joshua explains. "If we do this on a consistent basis, we begin to collect enough real-time observations to provide us a clear picture of how positively individuals handle change and interactions, the depth and breadth of their understanding of current processes and interactions with other processes, and how actively engaged they become, either through providing insight and ideas from an individual perspective or stepping up and asking questions to help lead others through the process."

"Creating Observable Leadership Moments©"

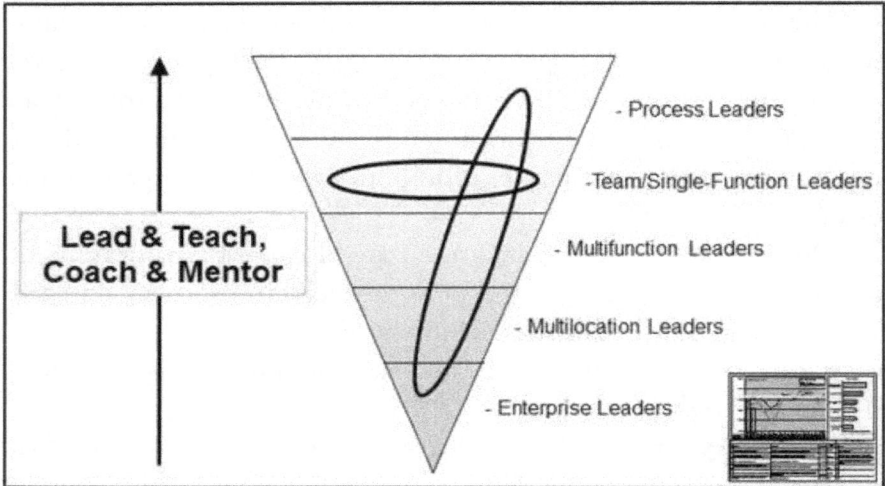

- Process Leaders
- Team/Single-Function Leaders
- Multifunction Leaders
- Multilocation Leaders
- Enterprise Leaders

Lead & Teach, Coach & Mentor

JC Bridge Builders © 2013

"I like what I'm hearing," Kate says. "I never thought about using the time we are engaged in the leadership process to observe how people are leading. I was only focused on improving the process and performance."

"When we use the leadership process this way, people who want a chance to show their leadership ability have a consistent opportunity to do so, leaders and organizations get the needed historical data for having meaningful succession-planning discussions, and current leadership gains predictable and expected opportunities for coaching and mentoring," Joshua explains.

"I get the first two parts, Joshua, but what do you mean by coaching and mentoring?" Kate asks, a little confused. "I though those things were only for executives, especially mentoring."

"At a simple level, coaching is helping people to know how to complete a task or portions of a task," Joshua explains. "Mentoring is helping people to decide what to do with the knowledge and experience they have in order to complete tasks."

"OK. I understand what you're saying, but can you give me an example of each for the leadership process?" Kate asks as she takes a drink of her iced cappuccino and takes another small cup of the yogurt and granola.

"When we use the leadership process, we can provide coaching by pointing out which questions to ask and when. For instance, before we ask for ideas to make the process better, we can demonstrate to those new to the process the need to determine how the process is doing over time and to identify one or two major factors that are preventing the process from meeting our goals. We can mentor people who are engaged in the process and interested in leadership by offering to help them decide what they would like to do with their ability to ask good questions at the right time, such as moving into a leadership role with more scope."

"Looking at coaching and mentoring that way, I see how the point-of-use leadership process would give us a lot more opportunities to coach and mentor at every level of the company," Kate says.

"You're right, Kate. To create a learning organization, both are needed by everyone at every level," Joshua offers. In a management model, as we talked about earlier, your knowledge is what got you promoted and kept you at the top. Your job was to find others with knowledge and have them come work for you. The more knowledge you accumulated and stored, the more power and control you had to keep things the way they were."

"You mean like a pyramid scheme or a pyramid of power," Kate states, connecting what Joshua had shared with what she has seen at work.

"Something like that, although I'm confident that that was not the intent in the vast majority of situations. But as a leader, each time you get promoted you have more people whose success you are responsible for. So you end up at the bottom of the pyramid, helping everyone above you learn how to be successful. You have to give away as much of your knowledge and perspective as possible to help them to achieve success."

Kate smiles and lets out a sigh of relief. "Finally, I have a way to not only see Frank or others in a leadership role, but I can also plan when I'll see them and be able to coach them on how to be better leaders, which should significantly improve the learning curve for becoming a leader. And if Frank or some of the others are interested in a leadership role and I become aware of that interest, we can have good mentoring discussions about the opportunities they have now or could have with further development."

"That's good to hear," Joshua says. "You mentioned improving the learning curve for becoming a better leader. How is learning handled at your company?"

Kate sits up and shifts in her chair as she notices the change in the direction of the conversation. "For the most part, we have a lot of training going on," she tells him. "In fact, we are going crazy trying to get all the requested training in. If it isn't technical training for a new system or method, it's development training for supervisors and managers." She pauses a moment and then frowns. "Now that I think about it, we spend a lot of time training, but I'm not sure it always helps the way we want it to."

"Let me ask you this, Kate: since we've looked at the integrated point-of-use leadership process and the multiple outcomes that are possible, do you know if your approach to training is integrated?"

Kate pauses to think. "I think I understand what you're asking," she replies slowly, still thinking it over. "Based on our conversations about the leadership process and my experiences with it, when I compare it with our training efforts, I'm pretty sure we focus on training and then applying that training to the job instead of doing both at the same time." She looks up at Joshua. "But I would like to look around and ask a few questions first."

Joshua nods. "That sounds good. We can pick up the conversation next week, and you can tell me what you found out." He stretches and stands up. "For now, why don't we go out to the kitchen and grab a bite to eat?"

"Aha, so you do still eat supper," Kate jokes as she gets up out of her chair.

"I said I was a little challenged," Joshua shoots back, smiling. "I didn't say I was abstaining."

Chapter 7 Work

As Kate and Frank are sitting in the cafeteria eating lunch, Kate suddenly looks up and asks, "How do you pick the person who's going to replace you?"

Frank's eyes widen. "Well, that's out of the clear blue sky. I thought we were friends," he replies, feigning concern but remembering that Kate had mentioned earlier that she wanted to talk to him about a promotion.

Kate grimaces. "Not that kind of replacement," she grumbles. "Like when you get promoted or decide to move to another area."

"You mean I'm getting promoted to a new department?" Frank asks with a big smile and an exaggerated amount of enthusiasm.

"Thanks for the help, Frank," Kate says sarcastically. "What I mean is, have you done any succession planning? You know, where you look for people who are promotable?"

"Are you kidding?" Frank responds, settling down with a realistic tone. "As busy as I am, Kate, I rarely get the chance to see—much less look for—anyone doing the things that I think a manager or leader does."

"Really?" Kate asks. "No one?"

"It's not that I don't think some of them could do the job or that maybe some of them already are doing the job, but I never get to see the proof. All I get to see are the end results, which just isn't enough."

Kate nods. "Well, I hear you there. I have my own reasons why it isn't enough, but why does it bother you?"

"Well, like with Julie," Frank says, "she really helps a lot in getting ideas from the group and getting things done around the area, but I don't really get to see her in action too often, if ever. It's been kind of like voodoo or something. I ask for it, she waves her magic finger, and the next thing I know, it's all better. I'm sort of hoping not to find any dead bodies lying around somewhere."

"Frank," Kate protests and starts laughing.

Frank smiles. "OK though, seriously, maybe if I saw her in action more than once or twice a year, I could give better input on how much she knows and how she does her magic." He sighs. "Right now, I'm willing to stand up for her to be one of our new leaders because I know she can get things done and her people really like working for her. But I'd almost be guessing on how she does it. Is this a Joshua thing again?"

Kate nods. "What if I told you that I know a way to fix it so that you *can* see Julie—or anyone else you wanted to see leading a group—as often as you would like?"

"That'd be great," Frank says. "So how does this newfangled process work?"

Kate takes a few minutes to explain to Frank the observable leadership moments that are created while using the leadership process and the links to succession planning. "So what do you think?" she asks when she's finished.

"Dumber than a biscuit, but happier than a clam," Frank says, smiling.

Kate pauses in surprise for a moment. "OK…those are new, cowboy," she says. "What do you mean by that?"

"Well, dumber than a biscuit because I see how easy it could have been to identify people to promote. And happier than a clam? Have you ever heard a clam complain, Kate? They hardly ever open their mouths to say anything, but when they do, it's a pearl."

Kate begins to laugh.

Frank continues. "We're always saying what people can't do, but now I have a way to say and show what they can do. I've had almost nothing that could prove how good they are for a long time, but now I can plan to collect all the data I need during the year so I can brag about how good my people are. I expect that I will have lots of good pearls to share, especially about Julie."

"You know, Frank," Kate says, calming down a little, "every now and then, your logic just scares me. But I like it. Would it be OK if we asked Julie what she thinks of the idea? And—if she likes it—whether she would be willing to help us set up a trial in her area?"

"Based on the conversations I've had with her and the way she works with her people, I think she'd be happy to help," Frank says.

"All right, then." Kate stands up and grabs her trash. "I think I'm gonna head back to my office," she says.

Frank nods. "I'll call you and let you know when Julie's going to stop by."

"OK, see you then." Kate throws away her garbage and starts heading back toward her office. As she does, she smiles, realizing that she is feeling better about work than she has in a long time.

Chapter 7 Home

"You know, Amber, I've been watching how you have been handling problems and making decisions lately, and I want you to know that I'm proud of how you are doing," Kate tells her daughter as they sit down at the kitchen table. "And you seem a lot more relaxed, too."

"Thanks, Mom," Amber says. "Up until just a little while ago, I didn't think you guys—or anyone—noticed what I was doing right. And knowing what everyone wants from me makes it a lot easier so that I can relax."

Kate smiles warmly at Amber. "You know, sweetie, I like that we're getting to talk with each other more often, and without the conflict. I don't think we talked enough in the past for me to be able to say whether you were getting better or worse, and so I feel like I shot from the hip a lot."

Amber nods. "Well, if we're in a confessing mood, I must say that I didn't know it could fun or enjoyable to be a leader. I thought it was going to be more of the same old same old. It's great to know what to do, whether it's knowing what I need to do to get ready for college or helping my friends when they have problems. Just knowing that I'll be able to help people I care about is exciting and feels great."

"I'm really grateful to hear that you feel like you know how to help," Kate says. "And, more importantly, that you want to, too."

"Thanks, Mom."

Kate nods. "Now, speaking of exciting, what are your plans for next weekend?"

Amber grins. "I'm glad you asked."

"Uh-oh," Kate says. "I know that look. Should I be sitting down for this?"

"You're already sitting down," Amber says, smiling. "I wanted to ask you and Dad if I could something a little different next weekend."

"What do you want to do, sweetie?" Kate asks.

"I would like to go with my best friends on a practice run for our senior spring-break trip."

Kate frowns and starts to tense up. "What do you mean?"

"We would like to go to Water World for the weekend, stay overnight on both Friday and Saturday, and then be home by three on Sunday," Amber quickly explains. "It's only about an hour and a half away, and we thought it would be a good place to try a trip together to see how it would work. Since it's close by, if we run into problems we didn't expect and need to make adjustments or ask for help, we wouldn't be too far from home. Plus, we have enough money saved up, so it wouldn't cost you a thing, and it would be better for us to learn now, instead of when we're so far away during spring break."

Kate smiles. "That was very well practiced, my daughter."

"Thank you. It only took three hours standing in front of the mirror."

"Did I agree to spring break?" she asks, teasing.

"Yes, you did," Amber says matter-of-factly. "In fact, you have a large sum of money that I gave you each week for it."

"I thought that was my tip for being a great mom."

"We have a plan," Amber says, continuing her sales pitch, "which includes contacting you and Dad as often as you need. I know it's a big step for you two, but I think you're ready," Amber digs at Kate. "I have the plan with me so I can show it to you if you want."

Kate nods. "Let's see it." It takes a few minutes for the two of them to get through Amber's plan, and Kate asks a few clarifying questions along the way. Afterward, she shares her feelings with Amber. "You know, sweetie, if you had asked me a while ago, the answer would have been absolutely not."

"So the answer's yes?" Amber asks excitedly.

Kate holds up her finger at Amber. "Let me finish." Amber nods happily. "Since I've seen how you've been handling yourself at school and home lately, and I've seen how you're approaching this trip, I'll be happy to support you when you discuss this with Dad. And while I think he'll have a few questions, I also think he'll be impressed with how well you and your friends have thought this through."

"Yay!" Amber squeals and plows into Kate with a hug. "Thank you, thank you, thank you!"

Kate laughs. "You're welcome, you're welcome."

Amber lets go of Kate and sits back down in her chair. "You know, Mom, without all of our talks and you teaching me about leadership and how it works, I don't think I would have had the chance to be able to show you what I could do. And I'm sure that I wouldn't have asked the right questions with my friends to be able to get good information for the trip."

"I think I'm grateful!" Kate says with a playful smile. While she is enjoying the moment, a thought strikes her. "Amber, have you considered leading one of the younger groups at church?" she asks. "There's an opening in the youth-leadership program, and I think you're ready for it."

Amber considers the idea for a moment. "You know, Mom, I think that sounds like a good idea. Though when I move on, who are you and Dad going to teach?" she teases.

Kate thinks about that for a moment. "I hear the elders have been looking for some young blood that can keep up. Maybe it's time for your father and me to get some coaching and mentoring from them. You know they say you're never too old to learn."

"And I'm sure Dad will be happy to know that you said that he's old and belongs with the elders," Amber says jokingly.

Kate laughs. "What's that? You say you want to present your idea to Dad without some wonderful Mom support?"

"Thanks, Mom, I knew I could count on you," Amber says as she heads toward the living room, looking for David.

CHAPTER 8

Overview

IN CHAPTER 8, Joshua asks Kate what types of training her organization has been using to develop engaged leadership and performance improvement. Through their discussion, Kate realizes that by separating the two types of training, they have significantly limited their ability to be effective at improving either. Joshua offers Kate a training model, one that aligns with the point-of-use leadership process for developing leadership and achieving business-improvement objectives simultaneously.

CHAPTER 8

Training-Systems Model
To Divide and Conquer...or Not—That Is the Question! Creating Real-Time Training ROI at Every Level, Every Time

"HI, KATE," JOSHUA says as he opens the door. He gives her a hug and then lets her inside. "Hope you had a good week."

"It was a great week," Kate says as Joshua takes her coat and hangs it up in the closet. "I'm looking forward to sharing some of the high points."

"That sounds great Kate. To help save some time, I put out a Danish that a friend has just sent us. It comes from out of state but it tastes like it was just made. I also put out a plate with several different choice for putting a salad together next to a pitcher of iced tea."

"Both of the food choices look really good Joshua. Thanks for giving me such a tough decision. Are we still filling out the chart? That might influence my choice!" Kate says as she smiles and makes her shelf a salad.

"No chart this week unless you want me continue! Joshua says smiling. I just want to make sure we are still friends!"

"Of course we are as long as you continue to listen to Lisa's advice on how to feed your friends!"

"Done deal! Moving forward while it is going great, you mentioned you wanted to share some of the high points of the week. Sounds like a great place to start," Joshua says as the two make their way over to the living room and sit down. "You go first."

"Well, for starters, thanks to using the point-of-use leadership process and understanding how it creates observable leadership moments, Frank and I were able to plan and observe our employees as they were engaging in leadership."

"That's good news, Kate. And was it helpful?"

"It was great," Kate shares excitedly. "We set up a trial in Julie's area with the leadership visual, and after we explained how it worked, we agreed that we would use it for the next four days. During that time, we were able to coach our individual process owners and supervisors on how to use the questions, which they caught on to and liked much more quickly than I expected. If fact they commented that they wish we had just said or shown them what we wanted a long time ago. And we were also able to collect some very good observable leadership moments for the ones who participated in and led the process."

"Sounds great. What were the results of the discussions?" Joshua asks.

"Very positive?" Kate offers hesitantly, knowing that she just shared how it went during the week. "What do you mean? 'Cause I think I just said how positive it was."

"There are always two parts to training, Kate," Joshua explains. "One is developing leadership, and two is improving performance to a goal. It sounds like you made great progress on the leadership side. I was just wondering how it translated to performance improvement."

"Oh, that part! Yeah, we actually reduced the downtime on one of the major jobs Julie runs in her area. Would you like to hear how we did on the succession planning?" Kate says, still excited.

"Of course," Joshua says, smiling.

"The observable leadership information we collected during our conversations gave us the beginning of real data that will really help us to have meaningful discussions during our succession-planning meetings in the fall. Finally, we can connect *what* was accomplished with *how* it was accomplished. And for the people who have been expressing an interest in leadership, now that we have seen some of them in action, we are planning training sessions for them later this summer."

"Sounds like you got a lot accomplished," Joshua replies. "Do you know what type of training you're planning?"

"Well, at this point, it depends on who it is. Some will be receiving technical skills training, and others will be scheduled for leadership training," she answers. "Now that we are starting to know our people better, we have a much better chance of providing the right training."

Joshua nods. "Did you get a chance to look around and ask questions about whether the training you are providing is integrated in its approach?"

"Molly, our human resources leader, was out all week, so I will have to catch up with her sometime this coming week. On my own, I was able to look at the outline of the courses that we currently offer, and I got a chance to talk to a couple of our in-house trainers for a few minutes. Based on what I could gather, it appears that our training is separated into technical training and leadership training," Kate tells him.

Joshua nods again. "OK." He thinks over what he's going to ask for a moment. "Well, first let me say that it's good to hear that your training is going to be better aligned. That's always helpful. So let me ask you a question in a slightly different direction. *Why* are you providing training?"

"To help our people be better at what they do?" Kate asks tentatively.

"So you are a people-development company?" Joshua asks.

"Why does my head sometimes begin to get fuzzy when you start asking me questions, Joshua?" Kate jokingly complains. "I mean, I like the questions you ask, but sometimes…" She shakes her head and sighs. "Well, anyway—no, I know that we're not a people-development company. But why are you asking?"

"Many times, our training efforts are very singular in their approach and are focused solely on developing the participant's understanding and knowledge during training," Joshua begins to explain.

Kate frowns. "Which is bad?"

"It's not necessarily bad. It's just that that approach isn't the most effective or beneficial way to train," Joshua answers. "To provide the best outcomes, we should be focusing on not only developing the technical skills or leadership ability of the person in the training, but also improving organizational and individual performance at the same time."

"Doesn't training provide the knowledge and skills that we want them to use on the job?" Kate asks, confused. "I took a look at the types of training we provide, and even though they're not integrated like the point-of-use leadership process, it seems like the trainees should be able to go back to their jobs and apply what they learned to improve themselves and the business."

"Providing training with the hope that it will someday make a difference may not be the best way to develop people or improve a business," Joshua says, a smile tugging at the corners of his mouth.

Kate smiles. "OK, good point," she says.

"The challenge to providing training for the future is that when we try to apply what was learned in training to the business or our jobs, we find that what we remembered works much differently in practice or in a controlled environment than it does in the workplace," Joshua says. "Another challenge is that as more time elapses between the training and when it's applied, the delay begins to cause gaps in the implementation due to interpretation or how it was remembered—if it is even remembered."

Kate nods. "Fair enough," she says. "I've had those things happen to me more than once."

"A third issue we face is that when we provide technical skills to help improve a process but don't provide the leadership skills needed to help lead the change effort, frequently the final outcome is that the improvement method doesn't get a chance to work because of a lack of buy-in," Joshua says.

"That happened a lot in our early performance-excellence efforts," Kate says. "So how would you suggest we train?"

"In our experience, whenever we provide training—whether it's for performance improvement or leadership development—it needs to be linked directly to improving business or organizational performance," Joshua tells Kate. "And at the same time, it needs to provide the development of individual leadership needed for helping a group to move from an unwanted current state to a better future state."

Kate smiles apologetically. "Could you give me a couple of examples to make sure I understand it clearly?"

"Sure." Joshua shifts in his seat to a more comfortable position. "If we have identified the need to improve organizational performance, such as a group of processes for meeting schedules, then we need to teach the technical skills needed to understand and improve scheduling processes, along with providing and teaching a leadership process for successfully engaging the process owners and key stakeholders to achieve a successful implementation.

"From the leadership perspective, if we've identified a need for improved leadership, such as the capability to communicate effectively, we need to identify the projects and processes where poor communications are causing poor performance and include improving the processes in the training. In this way, we integrate and apply the coaching and mentoring needed for the development of better communications for the individuals in the training while improving the process performance for the organization at the same time."

Kate nods. "OK, I think I understand what you're saying," she says. "In either case, whether we are focusing our training on improving leadership or improving processes in the business, we need to combine achieving the goals and objectives of the company with the development of the leadership that our people and organization need."

"That's it exactly," Joshua says. "It requires us to align our training with our business needs for improving, and there are many positive outcomes—one being that most often we are able to show an immediate or near-term return on our investment."

"Which every organizational leader wants," Kate says.

Joshua nods. "A second outcome is that our people are able to work on real business issues and get to see and experience how the methods work in real business situations. And a third outcome is that it gives us a chance to mentor and coach them on improving their capabilities, while also improving the business at the same time." He grabs the chart he brought from the end table next to the couch and puts it on the coffee table to show Kate.

"What's this?" Kate asks as she leans over the coffee table to get a look at it.

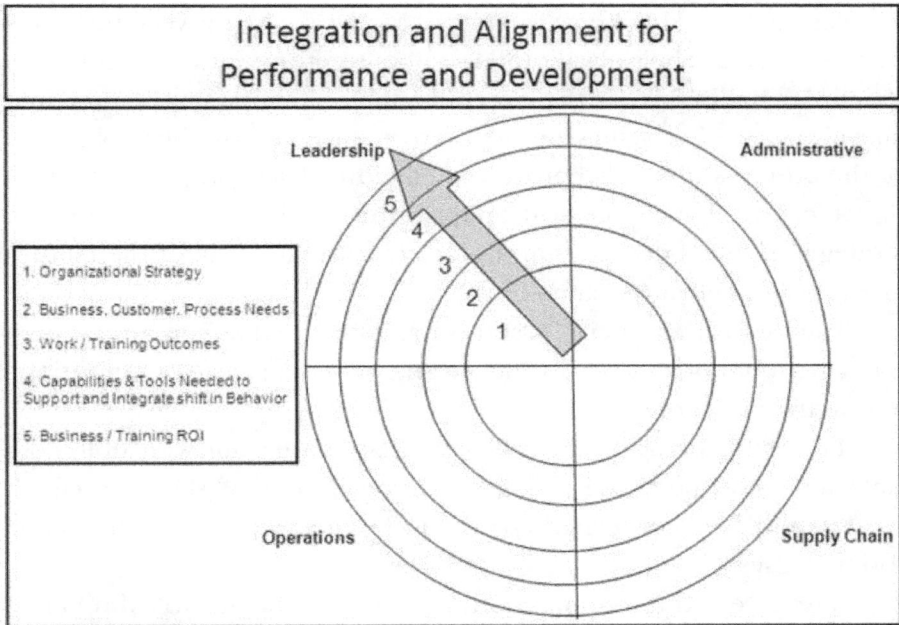

Integration and Alignment for Performance and Development

1. Organizational Strategy
2. Business, Customer, Process Needs
3. Work / Training Outcomes
4. Capabilities & Tools Needed to Support and Integrate shift in Behavior
5. Business / Training ROI

Leadership · Administrative · Operations · Supply Chain

JC Bridge Builders © 2013

"This is a training model that shows how we can align organizational and performance needs with the need to develop leadership capabilities while also providing an immediate return on our training and development," Joshua explains.

"So what you're saying is that we have to help them help us," Kate says as she looks the chart over. She sits back up and smiles. "What we need is for our training to show us the money, right?"

Joshua smiles. "Well, that's one way to look at it, Jerry Maguire Junior. But it's not necessarily about the money," he says. "If we work on the right leverage points, whether our business needs are to increase capacity or reduce costs, we will be able to significantly improve our ability to achieve success through deploying our training with the intent of improving the business and developing the leadership capabilities of our people at the same time."

Kate grins. "You know, I believe Molly would be very interested in this, Joshua. She's always talking about getting human resources a great leadership role at the executive table. I think that if they were actively involved in achieving the performance and financial objectives of the business while also providing employee leadership development, it would give them some real opportunities to influence some of our strategic business decisions and possibly leverage some of the cultural changes we need at the same time."

"I agree with you there," Joshua says. "I believe that human resources has a great opportunity to influence and help us achieve organizational and individual success."

"I'm really looking forward to having that conversation with Molly now," Kate says almost giddy. "OK, one last question for the day," she says excitedly.

"Should I be concerned about you bouncing off the walls, Kate?" Joshua teases.

Kate waves off the remark and takes a deep breath to calm herself back down. "You know that I have always had a significant interest in helping people and that I have spent time a lot of time working with Human Resources groups. And so my question is; I really like the idea of achieving more than one objective at a time, but will providing integrated training really help us to remember the training more effectively? One of the challenges we have faced in the past was that much of our leadership training never really became a part of what we did daily."

"That's a really good question," Joshua says. "In part, the answer is yes, because as we engage more of ourselves in the immediate application of the training, we learn and retain the information and skills much better, like learning to speak a foreign language in its native country instead of learning in a classroom and then trying to use it when we go to visit a country that speaks the language. However, also like learning a foreign language in its home country, the leadership and performance-improvement skills we learn need to be useful not only at work, but in every environment, including at home and in the community."

"Why's that?" Kate asks.

"Because if the leadership process we provide for decision making and problem solving is not translatable or usable in the environments where people live or does not resonate and align with what people think and believe and are experiencing daily, then it loses its credibility and ultimately its value and impact and will be discarded or quickly forgotten," Joshua says.

"Ah," Kate says. "So is that what you meant last week when you mentioned how the point-of-use leadership process is not only for work, but for home and the community as well?" Kate asks. "It sounds like a matter of scope again, Joshua."

Joshua smiles. "It *is* a matter of scope, Kate," he affirms. "If we can share a leadership process with our community, schools, and families in a way that provides the help and assistance they need while also providing them with positive interactions and success, then those capabilities and methods will become reinforced through practice and success in those environments as well." Joshua scoots to the edge of his chair, his eyes lighting up. "Leadership then becomes a way of thinking and a cultural approach to helping. In the long run, we won't have a shortage of good leaders when we need them, whether it's at work, home, or in the community, for all ages, backgrounds, and experiences."

Kate smiles at Joshua as his passion for people and leadership becomes apparent. "Now who might start bouncing off of the walls?" She asks teasing Joshua.

Joshua sits back, smiles, and shares a relaxed moment with Kate, not at all ashamed of letting his passion show.

Kate sighs as the full weight of the past couple of months catches up to her. "It's a lot to absorb and process, Joshua," Kate says. "I've seen personally how a relationships inside and outside of business could improve almost overnight by focusing on how to help individuals and groups go from unwanted current states to better future states instead of focusing on what's being done wrong all the time. I can see a lot of areas where an integrated approach to training would help us to tangibly connect leadership with the activities and improvement efforts we're currently working on in the company. But beyond work and with my daughter at home, when I think about the community and church organizations I work with, we have approached improvement efforts from just one perspective at a time there too." she says thoughtfully. "I don't know if we ever thought about directly connecting our youth-leadership efforts with our outreach initiatives. That might be a real way to help both groups succeed even better."

"You look pretty comfortable with where we're at today," Joshua notes. "How about we follow up in a few weeks and see how all of what we've been talking about is working together?"

"Sounds perfect," Kate says. She stands up and stretches. "You know, I've enjoyed our conversations immensely."

"I've been enjoying them, too," Joshua says. "When I realized a few years back that leadership was about providing the help that we needed to be successful, it changed how I approached business and people." He smiles. "Next time, let's not wait so long before we get together and talk. There are other things I would like to talk to you about and get your perspective on."

"Oh, don't you worry about that," Kate says. "After all you've helped me to do, you won't be getting rid of me for a long time."

Joshua laughs.

Chapter 8 Work

When Kate returns to work on Monday morning, she heads to her office and pulls out the training plans for the upcoming year. As she looks them over, she sees that the list is divided into two parts: leadership and skills development. She decides to head over to human resources to talk with Molly.

"Hey, Molly," she says as she peeks around Molly's office doorway. "Do you have some time available so that we could talk for a little while?"

"Sure," Molly answers happily. "My schedule's always open for you. Come in and sit down." Kate walks in and sits across from Molly. "What's on your mind?" Molly asks.

"I wanted to ask you a few questions about our training," Kate tells her. "I had a discussion with a friend of mine over the weekend about leadership and training, and he offered me some interesting ideas that I would like to get your opinion on."

"Sure. I'm always open to new ideas," Molly replies, "especially when it comes to training. It's such a difficult area to get the results we want."

Kate explains the training-systems model that she and Joshua discussed, tells how it ties in with the point-of-use approach, and shows Molly the visual that Joshua gave her for the training-systems model. When she finishes, she asks, "Overall, what do you think?"

"Well, wow," Molly says, sitting back in her chair. "Give me a minute to take it all in." She takes a few minutes to think about what Kate told her. "Well, first of all, what you described with the model makes a lot of sense to me, and I can see how it aligns with the point-of-use leadership process that we've been working with. We've been working very hard to prepare our people for the future and to help create a culture of leadership in the company. But based on what I've just heard and seen, I realize that we have some real opportunities in the ways that we approach our training—not only through our planned training, but also on a day-to-day basis."

"How have we been approaching them so far?" Kate asks. "I mean, I help put together a list on an annual basis for the different types of training I feel my people need, and I took a quick look last week to try to understand how we train, but I'm not sure I really understand it since I haven't been involved with how it's set up or delivered."

"Well, ordinarily, when it comes to training, we've been providing either technical or leadership training, but we haven't included a project for improving the business in either one," Molly explains. "In the technical training, sometimes it's a given that they'll apply what they've learned directly to the process. But more often it's just like our leadership training, where we train them on a new topic and expect them to be able to use it later."

"In general, how do we convey the knowledge and capabilities that we want the leadership participants to use?"

"There are a lot of ways to provide new knowledge and skills," Molly replies, "such as presentations, handouts, and videos. Several times we've had experts on the topic come in and speak to the trainees. But to help convey the concepts in a way that may be better understood or retained, we try to get closer to a business experience, such as having them study business cases from other companies to see how they address the topic. Or we've had business simulations, where trainees work together in teams to figure out what they would do in a given scenario. But we have never crossed the line to actually work on the business. The only leadership group we indirectly approach with an integrated process is at the executive level, and that's only on stretch assignments," Molly finishes.

"How do the stretch assignments work? If you don't mind my asking," Kate says.

"Not at all," Molly replies. "Overall, once we've identified someone with executive potential, we put them through an executive educational-development experience. Our intent is to provide new knowledge and perspectives that are beyond their previous education and experiences and are designed to be helpful on their stretch assignment," Molly explains. "We then give them either a short-term job assignment that is a level or two above their current level of responsibility, or we give them a high-profile project that is either very in depth or has a broad scope of responsibilities. We look to see how well they handle the increased responsibilities and broader range of expectations, along with how they approach more complex interactions and analysis, at both at the process level and the personal-interaction level."

"That sounds pretty intense," Kate comments. "Do you get a chance to coach and mentor these people very often in the stretch assignments?"

"In the temporary assignments, it usually goes pretty well, as the projects or special assignments they're on usually have a lot of visibility, and their assignment efforts are pretty focused," Molly says. "Because of the high level of visibility, coaching and mentoring occur frequently. But that's not usually the case with the full-time positions: it goes pretty well at the beginning, but as time goes by, the day-to-day business sometimes takes over, and the coaching and mentoring can get lost in the shuffle."

"Do you think that having business projects in our training like what you have in the temporary stretch assignments would help with the learning process and give the trainers more opportunities for coaching and mentoring?" Kate asks.

"Absolutely, Kate," Molly replies. "In fact, I think it's a good idea and a possibility that we should pursue, especially in the way that you described it working in both training and in the day-to-day use of the point-of-use leadership process. How about if you and I schedule some time this week to look at our training and see what opportunities we can come up with? Also, if you wouldn't mind, after we take an initial look, I would like to share our ideas with my group to get their insights."

"I wouldn't mind at all," Kate says.

"Ultimately, we'll need to try this out with some of the executives and get their feedback," Molly continues. "And if it works the way that we think it can, we can develop a plan to roll it out to the rest of the organization. Do you have anyone in mind in operations that might be interested in helping us pilot this?"

"You know Frank would be more than willing to help," Kate says, "and he has Julie, whom he would like to involve with this as well."

"That would be perfect!" Molly exclaims. "Both of them have great reputations with the people they work with, and we know that each of them is close to being ready to move forward into new leadership positions. We'll need to invite them to the meetings to get their input as well. Will you let them know?"

Kate nods. "I'm excited, Molly. I've been looking for a way to help our operations people be recognized for their leadership abilities for a long time. Finally we have a way that helps them. And the best part is that it's also a way to help our whole organization. Thank you for listening."

"Thank you for coming in, Kate. I've been trying to figure out for a long time how to get the HR group at the executive-decision table," Molly says. "With the training-systems model, I feel for the first time that we'll be able to do that. Our approach has always been to develop our people to help the company be profitable while meeting our customers' needs, but our training approach separated us from the business itself. Well, maybe now we'll finally see an end to that. Thank you so much for bringing this by, Kate."

Kate smiles. "It was my pleasure, Molly. I'm looking forward to our working together."

Chapter 8 Home

"You know, Amber, I haven't been hearing much from you and Dad lately," Kate says as she and Amber enter the kitchen to get ready for dinner. "Is everything OK?"

Amber nods. "For the most part, it's been great. Every now and then, though, we struggle because I don't understand what Dad is trying to teach me about living in the real world."

"What do you mean?"

"Well, I know Dad is trying to help, but a lot of the time, I feel like I'm only getting half of the story."

Kate smiles apologetically. "Can you give me an example?"

"Sure," Amber says. "Lately, Dad has been teaching me how to use money so that when I go to college or start my own life, I'll know how to do it successfully. Sometimes he gives me a lot of great ideas—they really do sound great—but when I go to spend my money, I can't remember everything he taught me, and I get it all messed up. So then he takes me with him to the store and shows me how to do it, and the money turns out great. But we don't talk about what we're doing, so when we get back and he asks me if I understood what we did and why, I can't really make the connections between what he said earlier and what we did, and it doesn't usually go over too well."

"Have you told him this?"

"Yeah," Amber mumbles. She shifts uncomfortably in her chair. "He says we just need more time in training, but I don't know if that's such a good idea."

"Why's that?"

Amber shrugs and then sighs. "Sometimes he gets upset with me and frustrated with himself. We've done this a couple of times in the last year already, and each time it ends up about the same. I wish we could do something different," she laments.

"It would be great if I could somehow hear about it, and then do it, and then talk about it. I think it might help me remember it better. But with the way we're doing it right now, I'm doomed either way," she finishes, sounding discouraged.

"Have you and Dad tried doing both at the same time?" Kate asks.

"Do you want to cause twice the problems?" Amber asks. "I can go to Dad for that kind of crazy talk, you know," she teases, trying to lighten the mood.

"Great, trapped again between my two favorite people," Kate jokes back. Amber laughs a little. "I just feel that there's a solution that can help solve both problems at the same time," Kate offers.

"Does it mean that I will have to work twice as hard at twice the speed? Because I already have a job along with my school work now," Amber reminds Kate.

"Actually, it should make things a lot easier," Kate assures Amber. "If you remember, when we were talking about the questions and the visual, you were the one who thought they should be combined."

"I remember that. How quickly things come around!" Amber says with a look in her eyes and a smile that say she's just been had.

Kate smiles also. "It should help to cut the learning time in half. That way, you can start working on some of your college classes now so that by the time you're twenty-five or thirty, you can support your mother in a way that she wants to become accustomed to," Kate jokes, trying to look serious.

"And I think you should hold on to that dream for as long as possible," Amber shoots back. "In the meantime, although I get what you mean about combining them, can you give me a couple of examples? Otherwise, it's like listening to Dad and Uncle Frank talk about some new martial-arts move without seeing the action, and who gets that, right?"

"Uh, right," Kate says, thinking about how Frank had recently been trying to teach David some new move by just explaining. "Actually, I do have a couple of good examples for you," she says. "In the problem you brought up about learning finances with Dad, you were actually right on the money, so to speak."

"Punny, Mom," Amber teases.

Kate grins. "Anyway, like I said, you're right on the money by suggesting that after you and your father discuss the concepts, you should right away practice what you were told. Then, as you're applying the concepts, he can coach and mentor you while it's occurring, instead of waiting to see how you did and pointing out what you did wrong after the fact."

"That's exactly what I need, Mom," Amber says. "Do you think he would spring for the blue sweater?"

"Admirable as it is to integrate your experience with your father and your blue-sweater objective, let's stay on topic for just a little bit longer," Kate says, smiling.

"OK, fine, fine," Amber says, rolling her eyes playfully. "I was just trying to integrate!"

"In the martial-arts example," Kate continues, "when your uncle Frank is showing him something new, it definitely helps your father to hear about it, see it, and then practice the moves and be coached, all within the same session. Otherwise, he says that it feels disconnected and takes longer to understand."

"So it feels the same way for Dad," Amber says. "Maybe I should have Uncle Frank over before we shop. It might help me with the blue sweater."

"Way to stay focused on the important parts of the discussion, daughter of mine. How about we go find your father and see if we can arrange a different shopping trip—one where we would explain and then work through the finances at the same time? Maybe I could come along and help?"

"Thanks, Mom, but I just texted Uncle Frank to see when he'll be teaching Dad again," Amber says with a mischievous smile. "Maybe we could really integrate and do all three on the same day. I really want that blue sweater."

"Sure, sweetie," Kate says and then calls out, "David, Amber and I have something we would like to talk with you about. Do you have a few minutes before dinner?"

Amber laughs. "Traitor," she teases. "Just remember that your retirement dreams may be hanging by a blue thread."

Epilogue

As KATE PULLS into Joshua's driveway, she sees him relaxing in his chair by the window. Joshua turns and smiles and waves for her to come into the house. "Well, howdy there, stranger," Joshua says as she comes in the front door. He puts down the article he was reading and walks over to give her a hug. As he lets her go, he says, "I haven't heard from you in a few weeks. How have things been?"

"Things have been getting better every day," Kate tells him as she puts her coat away.

"That's great," Joshua exclaims. "Why don't you come into the living room and tell me about it? Lisa's here, by the way."

"Does she have any those amazing macadamia nut cookies she used to make for me lying around? That would be a treat," Kate says.

"I know how much you like them so I already made up a batch," Lisa calls from the kitchen. "I just need to pop them in the oven for twenty minutes. Think you can hold out that long?"

"I've waited much longer than that for one of your cookies Lisa. I will do my best to hold on for another twenty minutes," Kate calls back.

"I'll bring them out as soon as they're ready," Lisa tells Kate. "In the meantime, would you like some coffee? I have something new that I think you'll enjoy."

"Of course," Kate says. "I know I can at least trust *you* with food and drinks."

Lisa laughs. "One cup of coffee, coming right up. By the way, you should bring David along with you next time. That way, the four of us can hang out." Lisa comes out of the kitchen with a hot cup of coffee. "I'll send you home with some cookies for him."

"Thanks," Kate says as she takes the mug. "I'll make sure to bring him next time. And I'll do my best to make sure that some of the cookies make it home."

Lisa crosses her arms. "Oh, I see how you are," she scolds jokingly. "Just to be sure, I'll be sending the extras home with you in a separate container, and I will call to verify that all of his make it."

"I think they're safe Lisa. Joshua has been tracking how many snacks I've been eating and I feel like I can make it home without losing too many on the way!"

"Oh, he has?" Lisa says in a way that sounds like Joshua is in trouble."

"I was using the snacks as an example for using the leadership process? Joshua asks.

"That was dangerous ground but as long as your still friends, and it worked to help Kate, I guess it's OK." Lisa says winking at Kate and sitting down next to Joshua.

Joshua grins in relief and turns to Kate. "So, now that you almost got me in trouble, why don't you share with me what you meant when you said that things are getting better every day."

Kate takes a sip of her coffee and begins to explain. "You know, when I came here for our first talk, Joshua, I knew that we were supposed to be creating employee engagement and improving our performance at work. But we were truly struggling to achieve or sustain either of them. Since you and I have been having our talks, we've been able to implement and sustain several areas of leadership and performance improvement at the company. And, just as important, relationships have been changing too. It's like a brand-new place. You can see and feel the changes in the culture."

"That sounds great, Kate. So, in your eyes, how did the changes occur?"

"Once we understood that we needed to transition from management to leadership and had a clear definition of leadership, including empowerment, we were able to see how leadership was a matter of scope," Kate tells him. "And when we saw and understood that the performance-excellence methods were leadership processes as well, and that the tools and visuals were for collecting and organizing data from leadership questions, it became easy to integrate our business-improvement and leadership-development efforts."

"So how did the integrated approach help you?"

"It's been amazing," Kate says. "Point-of-use leadership provided us with a common problem-solving and decision-making process and language at every level, and building bridges of communication created positive interactions, which gave us a way to establish and rebuild positive working relationships. Simultaneously, it helped us achieve individual and organizational performance and objectives through providing an integrated road map for transitioning from unwanted current states to better future states."

"Have you been able to sustain the gains you've made in performance and leadership development?"

"Yes," Kate replies. "Because the point-of-use leadership process is designed to help maintain a focus on performance over time, it provides the perspective we need to maintain the gains that we are making through our performance-excellence efforts. And knowing that we can create observable leadership moments whenever we use the process gives us the opportunity to provide real-time coaching and mentoring. This has provided us with meaningful succession-planning data and is helping us to create the bench strength we need. And, finally, by helping us to ask the right questions at the right time, the point-of-use leadership process is ensuring the sustainability of the leadership culture we have wanted and needed for a long time."

"Sounds like your group has made some significant progress," Joshua says.

"It was a lot easier than I ever thought it would be," Kate says. "And the great part is that using this process has not only helped me at work—which I would have been happy with at the beginning—but it's helped out at home, too."

"What do you mean, Kate?" Joshua asks.

"I came here just to visit a friend I hadn't seen for a while, and I was hoping to just get a few pointers about work. But what you have shared with me about how to develop leadership and success has been just as helpful at home as it has been at work," Kate says. "When everyone sees that leadership is a process and is just a matter of scope, they all understand it the same way and can apply it to their lives, whether at work, at home, or in the community. I was able to provide Amber the help she needed to become a successful leader at home and in school, just as I did with Frank and the teams at work. I'm really looking forward to helping out with some of our local community organizations as well. They've been asking for leadership for a while, but up until recently, I didn't feel prepared to provide it."

"I know you'll do a great job, Kate. I'm glad I was able to help."

"It means a lot to me, Joshua," Kate says. "The integrated approach that the point-of-use leadership process provides is so helpful in so many ways and to so many different people and groups. I don't know why I couldn't see the opportunities before."

"I think, Kate, that maybe we're not always looking for opportunities from an integrated or combined approach," Joshua offers. "Many times we try to solve a problem from one perspective at a time. If we would look at the possible outcomes of a process as a group more often, I think we would realize that we don't have to have so many separate activities to accomplish multiple goals.

"Going forward, I feel that the greatest gains will be made through the combined efforts of different groups. We have made great strides in many individual areas and disciplines. If we are fortunate and willing, I believe we may get to see and participate in an era of integration where we will make significant strides and experience great success in many areas, including collaboration and understanding."

Lisa smiles. "There's my leader," she jokes.

Kate smiles. "I like the sound of that, Joshua—actually getting the chance to look forward for once, instead of just focusing on where I am."

"I won't tell anyone if you won't, Kate," Joshua teases, "but that is one of the outcomes of using the leadership process."

"I get to see the future? I could sure use that on Frank on game days," Kate says, grinning.

"Way to keep your feet on the ground," Joshua jokes. "That wasn't really the scope I was going for there, Kate, though that would be pretty handy. But as we begin to learn more about going from our current state to better future states, we begin to consider our next steps even before we are pushed toward the future."

Kate nods. "I think I'm finally beginning to understand the concept of a learning organization."

"How's that, Kate?" Joshua asks.

"Continuing to ask questions and understand more about going forward leads us to think about the possibilities of the future, which leads to asking new questions," Kate says. "If this happens with everyone, every day, we begin to learn naturally, and it becomes part of the culture of our organization."

"And with that, I know that not only will you be able to help Frank and your organization, but many others as well," Joshua says.

"Thanks, Joshua. I just want to be able to help the people I live and work with to be successful," Kate confesses. "The more the merrier, right?"

"Agreed," Joshua says. "So, do you have any other questions for the moment, or are we ready to celebrate? I smell the cookies and the coffee and have to agree with you that even though I am willing to wait longer if need be, the less time we have to wait, the better."

"I do have one last question for today," Kate replies. "As of now, the point-of-use leadership is really working great for us and we've made a lot of progress. But I remember a few weeks ago, while we were talking about the fundamental leadership questions, you indicated that there's a list of questions that furthers the development of leadership. Are we ready for that list?"

"Absolutely," Joshua says.

"I'm curious—does the list have all the leadership questions?"

Joshua shakes his head. "I don't believe there will ever be a list that gives us *all* the questions, but the list contains a sequence of significant and easily understood leadership questions that, if asked at the right time, can very much help us to clarify what needs to be known, understood, and done."

Kate thinks his response over for a moment. "So does it matter what questions we use? Can we use the performance-excellence questions, or would it be better to use only leadership questions? Or is it some combination?"

"It is important that each of the questions be structured in a way that integrates and provides the perspectives of leadership, process, and communications. If we omit one of the perspectives, we can easily create conflict, failure to improve performance, and generate poor leadership. Once we have learned the process and how the questions are structured, then we can begin to add additional questions we may want or need.

"How about if I give you the decision-making and problem-solving questions? Next week, if your schedule's open, I'll show you how the lists of questions are designed to work depending on the types of problems you need to solve and the scope of the decisions you need to make."

"Sounds like a great place to start," Kate says. "I'm looking forward to it. But, Joshua, I really have just one more leadership question for the day," she says, seeing Joshua's attention already starting to shift toward the kitchen.

"Sure, Kate, but are you really sure it's the *last* last question? I mean, I don't want to rush you," Joshua says smiling and trying not to look towards the kitchen.

"Can I interest you in following me to the kitchen for some just-out-of-the-oven, amazing-smelling cookies?" Kate says with a grin, getting up from the couch. "Because I can't wait any longer either!"

"Now *that* is a great leadership question, Kate," Joshua replies with a big smile on his face. "And the answer is yes!"

www.ingramcontent.com/pod-product-compliance
Lightning Source LLC
Chambersburg PA
CBHW031936190326
41519CB00007B/560